LEISURE BUSINESS STRATEGIES

What They Don't Teach in Business School

John R. Kelly

SAGAMORE
PUBLISHING

Publishers: Joseph J. Bannon and Peter L. Bannon
Director of Sales and Marketing: William A. Anderson
Director of Development and Production: Susan M. Davis
Technology Manager: Christopher Thompson
Production Coordinator: Amy S. Dagit

ISBN print edition: 978-1-57167-706-8
ISBN ebook: 978-1-57167-707-5
LCCN: 2012947435

Sagamore Publishing LLC
1807 N. Federal Dr.
Urbana, IL 61801
www.sagamorepub.com

Dedication

To the paradigm-makers and the paradigm-breakers who have jumped the traditional fences of their disciplines' research and theory to create a significant area of study. Over a half century ago, Joffre Dumazedier of France investigated the real lives of French workers. Since then sociologists have broken the original work-determination models to connect leisure with all kinds of immediate communities. Social psychologists found new elements of leisure experiences. Feminists demonstrated that women are much more than adjuncts of male leisure. All explored how leisure has integrity and centrality in multifaceted lives. Now I dedicate this book to those, including future students of economics and politics, who will ask the unsettling questions and take the risks of breaking every old consensus and trying new paradigms. In the field of leisure business, I suspect they will focus on experience, access to resources, varied cultures, and even questioning the investment focus on toys and technologies.

Contents

Preface

This book is a conversation about leisure-based businesses. There are texts that address the sequential functions of forming and operating such a business. The first was this author's *Recreation Business* (New York: Wiley, 1985). They take the process step-by-step from concept through business plans, formation, financing, accounting, personnel, and resources. For those without business school preparation, they are useful if incomplete. They begin and end largely with a business point of view.

This book is different. It begins with the social and behavioral science research that has been developed since 1970. The continuing question is "How does this research guide and direct the beginning and operation of a LB (leisure business)?" The unfolding of the conversation starts with how leisure is different from other goods and services and continues with a number of themes directed toward both the formation and the operation of such an enterprise. It is directed toward the entrepreneur and those who are involved in developing LB strategies.

There is another critical difference. Gradually invading conventional business school thinking is the field of "behavioral economics." Counter to the traditional assumption of rational decision making in choices such as purchasing and investing, an enormous amount of research has now demonstrated that many, perhaps most, such decisions are not analytical. Rather they involve leaps to action from sets of unacknowledged assumptions, associations, and biases. Fortunately, in 2011, Daniel Kahneman, who won a Nobel Prize in economics for his pioneering work, published a very readable entry into behavioral economics. This approach informs the analysis of many of the issues of leisure entrepreneurship addressed here. (See *Thinking, Fast and Slow*, New York: Farrar, Straus, and Giroux, 2011.)

To a degree, what follows is one side of an imagined conversation with a senior scholar who has studied leisure and its social contexts for four decades. Incorporating work in sociology, social psychology, economics and even a bit of politics, he leads the reader through a sequence of common and uncommon issues related to leisure business. As outlined in the "About the Author" page at the end, his dozen books,

100-plus articles and chapters, and research and consulting are one basis for the analysis. However, almost as important, I have been observing and thinking critically (outside the usual B-school box) for long enough to turn some traditional ideas upside down.

The beginning is that "leisure is different." The focus is on what a LB sells or rents: an experience. The crucial element is quality. And the decades of study have yielded quite a lot of insight into how leisure experiences can be raised to a level that will attract and retain clients.

John R. (Jack) Kelly
2012

1

Leisure Is Different!

Is leisure business a big deal? Isn't it just an adjunct to the real business of manufacturing and associated businesses of transportation, construction, housing, and maybe communications? Of course, there is now general recognition that "services" are areas of major growth, especially health care and services to the growing "senior" populations. But leisure and recreation? Aren't they just the "leftovers" after everything necessary and important is provided?

Not if you are seeking an investment opportunity ... or even a job. If the manufacturing sector of the U.S. economy is roughly 9% of the total, that leaves 91% for all those services. For leisure business, business that is based on what people choose to do for the satisfactions in the activity (Kelly, 2012), even narrow definitions yield estimates of well over $2 trillion a year in the United States alone. Furthermore, leisure spending in the market sector is estimated at 97% of the total, with public sector spending the small end of the total. Leisure business, then, is a very big deal with lots of opportunities. Add the international markets and opportunities in this truly global economy and society, and the case for importance seems self-evident.

And that is only by narrow definitions: sports, games, concerts, the arts, leisure travel, and home entertainment. What about all the space, design, and implements in the residence that are built and maintained for leisure purposes? What about the proportion of transportation expenditures and those symbols of the playing self such as cars, other "big toys," apparel, and eating out in themed or exclusive environments? It is no longer necessary to convince car manufacturers that they are selling status symbols, lifestyle identification, and just plain fun. The clothing market sells styles symbolizing play to be worn in other environments. Housing is chosen for access to leisure as well as to good schools. Parents brag about their kids' sports and arts accomplishments and devote lots of time and money to support the activities.

Enough already? This book is not about trivial stuff. All these venues offer countless opportunities for financial investment and for self-investment in economic engagement that is interesting and satisfying. The scales of leisure business (LB) are global and local. The capital requirements are gigantic for a destination resort and tiny for an equipment repair business.

Question: *Would a list of leisure-based businesses be possible? Would it run into the 1000s?*

Hint: Don't stop with lists of activities or environments.

How Is Leisure Different?

LB is not like selling refrigerators or servicing cars. The conventional approach to this market sector is to take the usual functions of business, especially entrepreneurship, and apply them in conventional ways. Of course, there is validity in this. But it is not enough! Failure to recognize the differences is a recipe for failure. So, this book is about *What they don't teach in Business School* ... or at least not very much.

Rule 1: No One Has to Do It

This is so simple and self-evident that its significance is frequently overlooked. When you sell a car, your product is necessary for functioning in most urban and rural locales. Getting to work, medical care, food suppliers, social events, and leisure venues usually requires a car. Everyone knows this. So marketing is competitive, not singular. Will you buy <u>this</u> car against possibilities of other new models, less costly used ones, or fixing the old one? Selling has to take alternatives into account, but not walking or biking for most households. The marketing context is similar for most goods such as food, housing, maintenance, and even health care. But not for leisure!

As the old saying about living too long goes, consider the alternative. The alternative for leisure engagement may be a different activity or location, that is, substitution. The substitute for golf may be just walking, a "good walk" not spoiled. Pickup basketball may replace weight lifting, or a picnic rather than a restaurant, recordings for a concert, a driving trip not a tour or cruise, or a nearby state park not a distant national forest.

The basic question is how can a business increase its drawing power?

There is the default alternative: watching television still takes over two hours a day for most adults. It is cheap and accessible, that is not trivial when most people have limited discretionary income and other demands on their time. More on this later, but it is important to consider the wide range of alternatives when planning a LB resource.

There is the ultimate alternative: just not doing it OR a substitute. After all, leisure engagement is a choice. At any given time, there may just not be enough attraction for doing something to overcome inertia. This is the fundamental theme of this book: LB has to be attractive. The basic question is how can a business increase its drawing power? How can satisfaction be increased and dissatisfaction be minimized? Remember, no one has to do it.

The old market economics formula was supply rises to meet demand. It assumes that the demand is there and business responds. For leisure, however, there may be no evident demand for a product. Obviously, if it doesn't exist, demand is immeasurable. And, again, entrepreneurs are not just trying to beat the competition for established markets with measured trends. New leisure isn't necessary.

The "revised" business formula is reversed: supply creates demand. John Kenneth Galbraith pointed this out decades ago, but some traditionalists still resist. It should be self-evident. What business can afford to invest in a new product unless they believe that with the attractiveness of what they want to sell a profitable market will be created? The first function of advertising is to announce a market opportunity.

So, a market is, or is not, created.

Supporters of advertising costs call this "education." A second function is to make the offering seem attractive. So, a market is, or is not, created. This revision is crucial for understanding LB. The opportunity has to be attractive, not just useful, and never necessary.

Other Leisure Business Rules

The fundamental Rule 1 is only the beginning. There are at least eight more rules (to keep it simple) that are essential for developing good leisure business investment and operation strategies. All are not exclusive to leisure, but all have some special characteristics in the leisure context. Some are primarily oriented to concept development, some to marketing, and some to management. Some apply to all three business functions.

What is common to all the rules is that in developing or operating a LB, you ignore them at your peril. Failure rates are daunting (see Chapter 2). In business and entrepreneurship courses and texts, the primary cause of failure is usually said to be insufficient capitalization, that is, businesses run out of money. However, I would suggest that they run out of money at least partly because they don't have enough revenue. And they run out of money because they do not attract and keep enough buyers for their product or service. Most basic, then, would seem to be the failure to develop and operate a business that attracts and holds a viable market. Again, ignore these planning and operating rules at your peril!

(Note that all the rules are just being introduced here and will be explained and illustrated further in the following chapters that provide fuller contexts.)

Rule 2: The "Activity Life Cycle"

The business concept of the "product life cycle" is familiar to business students. Any new product has an introduction, growth, peak, and fall back to near zero or to a "plateau" that yields an adequate market base. All products have limited growth due to stimulated competition, limits on use or cost, or, in some cases, their "faddish" nature. For investors, the trick is to know fads from viable demand. And remember, a leisure business is based on people "doing leisure."

Leisure activities all have the same pattern. They may be new or improvements in what is already available. They are introduced, are promoted, grow, peak, and fall back to some level. No activity or product just goes on growing without limits. All "straight line" forecasts of growth are wrong. No exceptions! Anyone who promotes the newest opportunity as limitless is either ignorant, over-enthusiastic, or has something to sell.

Rule 3: "Location, Location ... "

The old real estate rule applies to LBs, too. As will be analyzed more further on, "if you build it in the wrong place, they probably won't come." In fact, they (target markets) may not even find it. There are several variations to this rule depending on the distribution of potential clients, access, barriers, and how the business matches its activity base. The point, however, is simple: a good concept in the wrong place is liable to fail. A corollary is that the offering in the right place still needs to look attractive. What real estate people call "curb appeal."

Rule 4: "For Every Thing There Is a Season ..."

The island on which I summer has an effective summer season of about seven weeks. Efforts to develop secondary seasons have met limited response. Therefore, a primary question to put to any business proposal is "Can you make a profit in such a brief time?" The seasonal limit may be caused by varying temperatures, limited winter access, extended summer heat, or some access factors. It also works two ways. If the activity is outdoors, climate variations may rule. If indoors, outdoor activity competition may place limits. In any case, many (maybe most) leisure businesses have peak seasons of limited duration or at least peaks and valleys in demand.

Rule 5: The "80-20" Rule Revisited

Let me admit to a seeming contradiction in this book. On the one hand, there will be an emphasis on baseline statistics as a corrective to overly enthusiastic estimates, the "hopes and dreams" scenarios. On the other hand (note that I, too, am a "two-handed economist"), realistic markets may be hidden behind aggregate statistics. The very useful Statistical Abstract of the United States (available free online from your helpful federal government), offers estimated numbers of participants in a wide range of leisure **... realistic markets** activities, usually with trend information. **may be hidden** However, careful analysis of household **behind aggregate** survey data (Kelly & Warnick, 1999) has **statistics.** demonstrated that only 20–25 % of these participants engage in the activity with any regularity, even in season.

The 80-20 rule of marketing suggests that only 20% of most markets provide 80% of the buyers or clients. The proportion is about the same for leisure engagement and provides a necessary corrective to optimistic claims of potential markets. Of course, it is also true that the 80% may be the best targets to try to increase the market size.

Rule 6: Begin With the Right Numbers

This rule actually is derived from the previous rules. I will provide some examples later, but the fundamental rule is simple: Get the best and most reliable numbers you can find.

There is no substitute for good statistics on just about anything. Nor are interpretations necessarily complicated. (See "Bayesian statistics simplified" in the next chapter.)

One issue is "Whose statistics?" It pays to be skeptical even of what appear to be good hard numbers. Those whose own profits depend on selling a service, product, or investment opportunity may take quite decent numbers and arrange them to their own advantage. The oft-quoted rules of "follow the money" and "consider the source" call for asking the hardest questions you can of any so-called "facts." Numbers do not automatically produce science.

Rule 7: Specialization, or the "½ of 1% Rule"

Another partial contradiction to Rule 6 rests partly on the 80-20 rule and partly on the peculiar nature of leisure engagement. The right business in the right place may prosper based on a "minority" activity or a special environment. There are activities such as rock-climbing that, at least until the last few years, engaged less than ½ of 1% of the adult population. Such activities don't appear on lists or aggregate summaries. In some cases, they may be confined to special areas so that the successful businesses are clustered in a place such as Hood River, Oregon, for windsurfing. Or, the niches may be a sign of possible future growth, subject to the limits outlined in Chapters 2 and 4. Niche markets are often based on relatively small numbers with high levels of commitment and personal identification such as the "specialists" and "amateurs" described in Chapter 4. The point is that numbers are important in their social and economic contexts.

Rule 8: Quality Is *Everything!*

Rule 8, of course, follows from Rule 1. No one has to do it, so second-best will fail and mediocrity is a risky strategy. Sometimes price alone will capture a segment of a large market, but for start-ups and long-term growth, quality is central. If the experience isn't powerful enough to bring people back and to stimulate spontaneous word-of-mouth and person-to-person promotion, the likelihood of success is very small. The many elements of quality and the nature of positive experiences will be addressed in later chapters. But the central point is so basic to LB investment and management strategies that it recurs throughout the book.

Rule 9: Experience Is a Process

There are lots of survey instruments that ask questions about satisfaction. For the most part, they allow only summations: "Overall, on a 10-point scale, how satisfied were you with _____ the (cruise, motel, salesperson, or whatever)?" The problem is that your engagement at the fitness center, on the wilderness hike, or at the concert is a process made up of several components. Later the importance of the final phase of a leisure event will be found to have

. . . any experience usually has several dimensions that rise and fall throughout the process.

disproportionate weight in overall satisfaction. Now just accept that any experience usually has several dimensions that rise and fall throughout the process. A few "highs" may outweigh even common boredom. The factors that produce highs and lows will be introduced and examined in ways that suggest what to plan for in designing for satisfying experience.

> **Question:** *Are all the rules equally important or do they vary in salience for different kinds of activities and settings? Without looking ahead, which grab your attention and why?*

> **Clue:** The most important elements of satisfaction may not be the same for all kinds of leisure experiences. What activities and settings do you have in mind?

> **Hint:** You may be biased by your own history of engagement satisfaction.

Of course, "rules" are just perspectives or ways of looking at whatever you are thinking about. (The technical term is "heuristic devices.") What is different about the following chapters is that they do not rest on conventional business or economic assumptions but rather on some psychological, sociological, anthropological, and other social/behavioral science research and approaches. Cross-disciplines such as behavioral and sociological economics will emerge as basic. The rationale for this is the nature of what the business is attempting to sell, a quality experience worth paying for.

Why Is the Approach Useful?

It provides analysis grounded in human experience rather than abstracted models. Practically, it offers one way to minimize failure and to beat the odds. It may also be the best way to develop the basis for experiences that attract clients and bring them back.

Let's take a closer look at this in the next chapter.

2

Thinking About It

Even such neat rules as those just introduced may be deceptive. When we get down to cases, thinking both critically and constructively may be harder than you think. This chapter gets us further into the process.

To begin with, creating business success requires more than enthusiasm and hard work. By a common estimate, close to 80% of new businesses fail within two years. "Good news" reports indicate that 35% are still in business after five years. In either case, the odds are against the entrepreneur. And there are no data or strategies demonstrating that leisure-based businesses have better odds.

There Are No Guarantees

Have you heard the claim, "This business can't fail!"? Of course, neither could "Mighty Casey" who, as you remember, struck out. Leisure-based businesses are subject to the same limits and problems as any other kind of business. Of course they require adequate capitalization, a carefully assessed market, access to clients and suppliers, competent bookkeeping, and well-chosen staffing. There are all kinds of issues that may bring down even a good concept in a good location. However, leisure businesses have that added warning factor that "no one has to do it."

The other side stems from the same source. Enthusiasm may spring from personal experience. However, really liking the activity base of a start-up does not always translate into success. There is always the downside of the "activity life cycle." There are cost factors. And "consider the source." If the claims of "great expectations" come from those promoting their equipment, franchise, or advice, then caution is advised. If those promising success will benefit from your investment, ask questions ... some of which follow.

The first is the basis of projected markets. Again, there are NO straight-line forecasts. I am always amazed how often self-credentialed expert consultants base their recommendations on projections that continue current patterns. For example, a tourism and second-home island hired experienced consultants to develop plans **... there are** for their ferry company, airport, and new **NO straight-line** school. All three based their plans on **forecasts.** straight-line population increases despite clear limits on waterfront development, market-cost parameters, demographic realities, and other factors. And that was without the emerging recession in hard-hit Michigan. We will return to realistic assessment of potential markets several times. Here let it suffice that there are always limits.

Are There Ways to Beat the Odds?

For those who want to challenge themselves, I recommend the 2011 book by Daniel Kahneman (Nobel Prize for economics in 2002) *Thinking Fast and Slow*. It is surprisingly engaging reading, perhaps because Kahneman is a behavioral psychologist, not an economist. However, for those not ready to take on the 481 pages, we will adopt several of his insights and perspectives throughout this book. The theme is simple: There are habits of making decisions that commonly lead to mistakes.

To compound the problem, those mistakes are most frequent when we are pretty sure of ourselves. The solution? Informed and critical thinking. We'll try to help.

Kahneman (2011) refers to countless studies that lead to the conclusion that there are two types of decision making, which he calls "System 1" and "System 2." System 1 is how we make most of our decisions most of the time. It is quick, often because we have to be. My usual example from flying is the unexpected and sudden entrance into zero-visibility conditions requiring an immediate switch to instruments and a decision as to the best course for getting out. Experience rather than flight manuals provides the basis for the necessary action, generally made correctly by those of us who are "old, not bold" pilots.

System 1 doesn't identify all relevant knowledge, calculate validity of information, and do a reasoned cost-benefit analysis and risk assessment. For most of life, it doesn't have to. For business decisions with long-term consequences, System 2, which completes all those operations, should be employed. Also, System 2 is required for criticizing and improving decisions that begin with System 1. The problem is that "System 2 is lazy." Most often, we have to make a real effort to employ System 2 (e.g., reading this book).

Perhaps surprisingly, both are relevant for this book. Understanding System 1 is really useful for understanding many leisure choices for potential clients and how to shape them. System 2 is necessary if you are to have a business that develops in ways that find and satisfy your markets. There are a number of perspectives unique or at least especially significant for a LB that help beat the odds.

Errors to Avoid

WYSIATI

The first, according to Kahneman (2011), he calls "WYSIATI"—WHAT YOU SEE IS ALL THERE IS. As with most of his themes, it is really very simple. It's a complex world out there. It takes a lot of disciplined effort to ferret out all the relevant information (data) on which to base an informed decision. So, mostly we just do a quick take on what we already see or think we know and then decide. It is "tunnel vision" that doesn't even see the tunnel. One common social-science slogan is that "it's a multivariate world out there." To make it worse, the world is an interactive system so that changes in one factor create changes in others. The world (for which in business read "markets") won't hold still.

To make it worse, the world is an interactive system so that changes in one factor create changes in others.

For example, let's say that 15% of the U.S. population over 17 plays golf. So, assessing whether a new golf development will find a market, you can begin with your likely population catchment area. However, there are other factors: Only about 25% of those who report that they "play golf" are on a course once a month or more. Golf is relatively costly, so you have to factor in pricing against your considerable investment. There are economic factors of unemployment rates, income distribution, and area projections. Of course, the "golf boom" has leveled off, but it has the unique sports element of retaining a high percentage of older players. However, some of them are moving south to gain a longer season. Then there is the growing "boomer" cohort entering retirement years in which they may enlarge the golf market. Conversely, this market may be limited by the low percentage who have saved adequately for a secure retirement

And so on and on.

It is easier just to look at courses in the area to see if they are crowded and make a decision based on "what you see" or even the difficulty you had reserving a tee time last Saturday. And, certainly don't factor in big elements such as recessions, the cost of gas, the impact of the housing market surplus on golf-based housing developments, and the participation trends that are not "straight line." After all, doesn't your enthusiasm count for more than all that complicated stuff?

Question: *How can this go wrong? An experienced gambling resort company is seeking investors for*

their new project. They have identified a half dozen "underserved" markets for establishing new casinos. You already know that gambling is a "money machine" for the operators since all the odds favor the "house" and profit margins are built into the structure of the development and operation. Is this surefire?

Clue: Look beyond "what you see." It isn't all there is. Further investigation of the industry will reveal a number of facts: First, all casinos do not succeed. Remote failing locations demonstrate the limits of the catchment area due to time and money travel costs. Second, there is new competition as more and more online gambling opportunities and formats become readily available. Third, each location will have its own set of regulations and demands for revenue-sharing. Fourth, it is difficult to start small when expectations for lavish venues are commonplace. Fifth, income and employment trends in the area may also limit the market. Some formats will tend to rule out the "high-end" market. All these and more components of a System 2 decision are relevant.

Corollary: What You Think You Know May Not Be Right

To use the same example, your little tee-time sample may obscure the fact that half the golf courses in the area are losing money or members or both.

As will be seen in Chapter 11 and elsewhere, there are many sources of data out there, often free. But all require interpretation. Interpretation requires context analysis. Context includes several interacting elements.

Here let it suffice to recognize the limits of personal perspectives. We all have limited experience. Probably more important, we view the world from a set of what have been called "domain assumptions." These are so fundamental that for the most part we don't even recognize their existence. You may believe that "free enterprise" always leads to growth.

You may believe that everyone really wants to be in outdoor environments. Or you may be sure that it takes competition to produce effort. Such assumptions are often too deep to be recognized and evaluated.

Sometimes we react with strong emotions to an observed action or even a single word without knowing just why. We may have experienced a violation of how we define the world that rocks us to our core. That is, it challenges or even violates some domain assumption. Do you value schedule over flexibility, time at home over time with "the guys or girls," work over play, or regularity over spontaneity? Any of these may bias a business plan.

The problem here is that these premises shape how we look at the world, what we see, and our mode of interpretation. We try to make sense of the behaviors of others out of our own world views. In marketing, we project on others the same kinds of meanings and satisfactions we have found in certain environments, actions, or associations. So, one of the purposes of social/behavioral science is to help us develop a more complete and critical understanding of why people run to the point of exhaustion, enter strange and even threatening environments, or stay home and tend their gardens. In developing a LB, we need such enrichment and correction of our own understandings

I Can Change the World

The third fallacy is the confidence that "I can change the world." The truth is that we can seldom even change the behavior patterns of one person. Witness the common failure of basketball coaches, especially young ones, who believe that their magic touch will change the selfish, arrogant, and self-aggrandizing play of a pampered high-school star into a mature college team player. Or, the restaurant purchaser who is sure that she can make a success in a location with a string of failures.

The moral is simply that PAST BEHAVIOR IS THE BEST PREDICTOR OF FUTURE BEHAVIOR. Of course, you can think of exceptions. Kids do mature. A shrewd market analysis can sometimes create business success out of former failure. But the starting point for anyone thinking about leisure business is there to see. What has been the history of such businesses? How do potential clients spend their time and money now? What are the most common traffic patterns in a city or resort area? With whom do your target markets spend their nonwork time?

This is why baseline numbers are a better jumping-off platform than hunches, flashes of insight, or the claims of enthusiasts. Of course, people do change ...

The moral is simply that PAST BEHAVIOR IS THE BEST PREDICTOR OF FUTURE BEHAVIOR.

sometimes. However, if the success of your business dream requires changed behaviors, begin with current behaviors and then look critically at what may bring about change.

Moneyball

This is why entrepreneurs need to learn to play MONEYBALL. *Moneyball* is the title of a film extolling the wonderfulness of a real-life baseball general manager who, to oversimplify, largely ignored the expert judgment of scouts, managers, and coaches in selecting minor-league players to nurture and advance in their system. The result was that a very low-budget team won a lot of games and beat out the big spenders in the playoffs. (From my bias, it is important to note they had very good pitching.)

Kahneman (2011) uses this story to pound home the importance of "base numbers." In the error of immediacy, decision makers commonly ignore the numbers. Investment strategies should always begin with whatever data are available on what potential clients do now, where they do it, what they spend, and, when possible, what they do NOT do. Can a new opportunity alter those numbers? Of course, but certainly not always and only when something powerful overcomes inertia.

A correlate error is overgeneralization from small numbers. Very localized data, one-time rather than trend numbers, and special cases may bias judgment. At the very least, beginning with the numbers on potential client-markets provides a base for developing realistic strategies. Current spending patterns suggest how allocations are made and where they might be altered. For example, average household spending on leisure stayed at about 8–9% for decades until some recent shifts (see Chapter 12). However, income levels and economic conditions have impacts. Leisure spending has general limits. Strategies to change patterns begin with the present.

. . . income levels and economic conditions have impacts.

"Bayesian statistics," developed by an 18th century English clergyman, is a model of how people change decisions when confronted with evidence. An example would be the likelihood that current participation in indoor fitness programs and measured dropout rates would be altered by a classy new facility. Without getting into the numbers at this point, there are two bases in Bayesian probability analysis. The first is simply that the base (current) rates are VERY important. The second is that mathematical calculation of the impacts of a new factor are generally much lower than personal enthusiasms would produce. Anchoring judgment in base numbers is a necessary beginning. (More on this later.) Furthermore, be critical of your own thinking. And recall that System 2 is usually lazy.

Problems such as WYSIATI and overgeneralization from small numbers are common errors in business development. "I have seen how those kids really love playing tennis, and the parents I have talked to would love to see a professional developmental program available." Ask how many kids and what else are they doing? (Baseline) How much are most parents able and willing to pay, and for how long? (Baseline)

Question: *Pick a business and develop three critical questions to ask.*

Clue: What would it take to change behaviors?

But Doesn't My Judgment Count for Anything?

Of course, in the end it's your judgment that really matters. After all, in most investment decisions, especially those in business start-ups, it isn't "just money." This is your life! As anyone who starts a business will tell you, especially at the retail service level, the demands on the entrepreneur's time, energy, and attention seem limitless. Probably there are aspects of the business that have appeal beyond profit. They may include location, association with congenial clients and staff, and the chance to do it "your way." Such side-bets are not trivial.

Then, what will the remainder of this book attempt?

First, we ought to be able to improve your odds. Most fundamental are perspectives that can help optimize the experiences of those who are paying for your services. We know quite a bit about satisfactions that ought to be integral to your operation.

Second, there is useful material on what motivates players, possible clients, to make leisure-oriented decisions. Call it "marketing" or call it understanding people, it may translate into attracting clients.

And, third, a bit of System 2 strategy. Talk to a good attorney about how NOT to "bet the farm" or your home or your retirement savings. The protections of limited liability formation and using OPM (other people's money) can reduce the personal risk.

At the time of writing, Western economies are deep into a recession that has no clear ending in sight. These are "tough times." However, for a new business, there are no easy times, so let's begin developing strategies that are realistic about obstacles.

3

INVESTMENT STRATEGIES FOR TOUGH TIMES

As previously suggested, for new businesses, all times are tough in some ways.

Does Business School Have the Answers?

Of course, conventional business and entrepreneurship analysis has a lot of wisdom that is not to be ignored. There are marketing techniques that have been successful. There are accounting practices that reveal problems. Failure to do good bookkeeping can even land you in trouble with the Internal Revenue Service and other taxing agencies' hot seats. There are business functions that no excitement or personal experience can neglect.

However, most conventional analyses I have seen locate the failure of new businesses in the lack of money. That is, "undercapitalization" causes new businesses to run out of operating capital as markets develop more slowly than anticipated. It is true, of course, that instant markets are unusual and that stable markets take time to nurture. So a realistic assessment of capital needs is necessary.

There is, on the other hand, another perspective on this issue. A business in trouble fails to attract and hold enough paying clients. For whatever reasons, the experience or product fails. Sometimes the root cause is in the concept, location, or some other foreseeable factor or combination of factors. In other cases, the business fails to provide an experience satisfying enough to retain clients and prompt them to bring along their friends. It is basic that person-to-person recommendations of current clients is the best form of promotion ... and the lowest cost.

Are There More Unconventional Factors for a Leisure Business?

Failure to Understand the Product

Remember, we are not selling a slightly improved microwave or more durable shoes here. All a LB has to sell is the experience. Therefore, promotion that is primarily comparative is unlikely to attract. Rather, in a LB, promotion has to focus on the quality of the experience. It may be thrill, comfort, companions, the environment, or learning. Therefore, knowing research on satisfactions and motivations is crucial.

All a LB has to sell is the experience.

Failure to Recognize the Unique Character of Leisure

For the moment, just review Rules 1 through 9.

Question: *Try to identify at least one example for each rule out of your own experience as a client.*

Hint: Some experiences may not have been ones you wanted to continue.

Failure to Think It Through

For example, if no one has to do it, then the competition may be out of sight. In usual marketing calculation, the competition is usually another supplier of a similar product or service. In a

LB, the competition may be almost anything that is available and may promise some form of enjoyment or satisfaction. Reading may replace a hike, an online game a movie, or a shopping mall a park. Furthermore, change is everywhere as will be explored later in this chapter. Markets won't hold still.

Avoid System 1 Errors: The "Halo Effect"

Kahneman (2011) demonstrates how the System 1 mind can be primed either positively or negatively by a word or two, a recollection of an event, or association with a warm and friendly companion. This priming produces a "halo effect" that can influence one's judgment on a current or anticipated experience. Obviously such priming is useful in designing promotion materials and advertising strategies. However, it can also lead to evaluations that are overly positive. For example, recalling a valued companion before assessing a leisure service may skew our judgment toward a false positive. The "halo effect" can be partly corrected by employing the *Moneyball* strategy of getting baseline numbers or getting a wide sampling of other users and clients.

Is Anything Important Simple?

Probably not ... certainly not an investment analysis. There are countless examples:

- A different location may also have a different set of cultures in the sought-after market.

- Weather aberrations can severely reduce visitors to a vacation area.

- Media attention to a new game or activity may prime a positive bias and evaluation. This has been called the "Olympics effect" as related to girls' gymnastics or women's soccer football. In both cases, most of the effect was temporary.

- Economic growth may involve gains in "productivity" relying on longer hours and greater pressure on the worker.

Numbers are important, but markets are more than numbers. As will be examined in the following chapter, there are many cultural and stylistic elements in leisure choices. Every male between ages 65 and 74 cannot be simply profiled as to favorite activities or satisfactions, even if most do watch TV sports.

Observation is a valuable approach to understanding what people actually do in relation to a particular resource and how they do it. For example, there may be more resting, socializing, and shopping than skiing at a resort that advertises its challenging ski slopes and powder snow. Furthermore, what we see is not all there is. Seeing what people do on-site may tell us little about the home-based small worlds where they make decisions to go to the recreation site or not. Histories of activity and skill investment are largely hidden and may be difficult to access. The point is that people are not just "skiers," "golfers," "swimmers," or anything labeled by an activity.

Then, There Is the Big World ... or, Why Macroeconomics Is Important

This is not the place for a detailed analysis of economic models. However, the big picture of economic shifts, trends, and processes impacts every kind of business. Globalization, recession, recovery, dislocations of production, distribution of income and wealth, scale of retailing (big box stores), distribution patterns (logistics, online orders, and subcontracting), and media shifts (from newspapers to the Web) ... all these and other big picture factors impact even the most local business. Financing, markets, costs of products, branding, and other local functions are affected by the larger economic movements.

There are also political macro-changes. In the United States an administration that invests heavily in environmental protection and natural resources for outdoor recreation may be followed by one that seeks to minimize government involvement in such areas. Such policies can make a difference in the quality and attractiveness of the resources that draw clients for secondary businesses.

Then, there is the reality of recession. By definition, "discretionary" spending may be cut or even eliminated in household budgets when there are reductions in household income. Increases in unemployment ripple through regions and nations with drastic impacts on leisure spending, both big ticket and immediate. Boats are abandoned rather than purchased. More vacations are taken in the car. Expensive opportunities are postponed. Even gambling is reduced by over 20%.

Income and Wealth Define Markets for Leisure

As mentioned earlier, the average of 8–9% of household income spent on leisure remained fairly consistent until about 1990. Then it crept upward only to be reduced by recession-related cutbacks. However, that is an average, either a mean or a mode. The distribution is quite another matter. The familiar "bell-shaped curve" applies here as to all distributions. Some households, usually due to low incomes or cultural prohibitions, spend almost nothing on leisure. Others, with higher incomes and wealth,

The point simply is that shifts in income and wealth, not just unemployment and poverty, help define leisure markets.

may spend 50% or more on leisure broadly defined. If the leisure space and equipment of homes, upscale travel with luxury and privacy, designer play togs, and "big toys" such as yachts and cruisers, vintage sports cars, lavish entertaining, and third homes in exotic locales are included, then the 50% figure may be low. Many of the wealthy are little impacted by recession. Some are, but spend anyway out of their surplus. The point simply is that shifts in income and wealth, not just unemployment and poverty, help define leisure markets.

When assessing business opportunities, the lure of "high-end" markets is hard to overestimate. The "lifestyles of the rich and famous" provide images of big spending that translate into big markets, or at least so it seems. It is true that recessions seem to have little impact on the leisure spending of the wealthy. There are always hundreds of expensive yachts for sale. However, most luxury tours and resorts do not close in tough times. The problem with concentrating a business plan on high-end markets is, of course, saturation. Others have noticed that the markets, while small in numbers, have held up well in a recession. Also, the very wealthy, the upper 1% or even 10% in income and wealth, may be less likely than those on a tight pleasure budget to cut every possible expense corner. Having noticed this, upscale resort developers pile investment on investment, and many find bankruptcy.

At the other end, the officially poor, as measured by the very inaccurate household income levels that ignore life circumstances such as persistent health problems and debts, are generally ignored in LB investment strategies. More recently, recession and unemployment have caused the government to discover a new category of those with very small discretionary incomes called the "near poor." The near poor, which includes the "working poor" and the officially poor, constitute up to 45% of the population. Their lives are precarious; they are less than three months from destitution if income is severely reduced or expenses are raised by an emergency. It does not mean that this enormous population segment is not interested in play, leisure, and diversion. But it does suggest that dollars spent will be limited and usually rationed carefully. A LB seeking new markets in the near poor will be competing with television and "big box" shopping, not a luxury tour or big toy.

Of course, one way of responding to the half of the population between the high and low is to cut costs. The danger is that the quality of the experience will also be reduced, making repeat visits or trips less likely. Perhaps the biggest challenge for leisure entrepreneurs is to find ways to offer a quality experience at limited cost. (More on this later.)

Government policies are also relevant here. Discretionary income is "after-tax" income. Levels of taxation in relation to income can shift spending. A major move from a progressive income tax to a VAT or consumption tax might make potential clients think twice about an expenditure. Dropping the income tax deduction on second homes would impact many vacation areas. Luxury taxes on expensive boats, or any boats over 15 feet long, would hit sales.

Nothing Lasts ... Except Change

No one has to be reminded of the power of technologies to change even ingrained habits related to leisure. The telephone made arranging events from household to household much more convenient. The car gave flexibility to leisure travel. The jet opened long distances to vastly expanded markets. Television transformed time use in almost every home. Now there is the home computer, online everything, and portable devices with new programs, apps, and connections almost every month. And clearly, all the devices and websites are not just for communication, information, and business. They are the new "sites" for fun, play, and leisure. The difference is that the opportunities go almost anywhere with the bearer.

> **The difference is that the opportunities go almost anywhere with the bearer.**

What will be the impacts of all the online activity on former leisure investments of time and money? Frankly, no one knows for sure. The enthusiasts claim that everything will be changed. The cautious remind us that deeply ingrained habits do not change that easily, at least for those over 25 and certainly for those big markets of the over 65.

How large is the online experience market? Note that in a decade, websites have almost eliminated local travel agencies, as even remote B&Bs have their own websites accessible simply by typing in the name of the nearest town. The technology expanded the B&B's market reach. It did not put it out of business. Some technologies enhance opportunities for other businesses. Remember how the interstate highway system, the car, and now Internet replaced old hotels with motel chains? The good news is that technologies have enabled all sorts of new LB opportunities. The bad news is that competition is no longer just local.

Question: *What new technology do you think will most impact leisure? Will its impacts open more businesses than it closes?*

Clue: How will it change (or not) how people live day to day? On special occasions?

Resistance to Change

Kahneman (2011) calls attention to the "endowment error." It operates on the behavioral level. By and large, people whose leisure is sedentary do not become physically active due to a new opportunity or activity. They go on watching television. Cultural patterns tend to change slowly, if at all.

However, the endowment error can also be a problem for businesses. A gradual erosion of a market may be unnoticed or explained away by an entrepreneur deeply invested in a particular activity base or locale. For example, if the owner of a camping site for RVs, trailers, and various campers sees his trade eroding, does he analyze changes in travel patterns, equipment investments, and the characteristics of his visitors or does he just put up a couple of new billboards assuming the market is still unchanged?

Cultural patterns tend to change slowly, if at all.

Endowment in the form of personal loyalty, habit, or unquestioned assumptions may cause bad judgment. Change is constant.

We will take a closer look at trends and fads in the next chapter. Here let us note a seeming contradiction: Change is everywhere and people don't change much. How can we reconcile that no market remains the same with the fact that "past behavior is the best predictor of future behavior." Is it a cop out to suggest that to begin to deal with this dilemma, it may be helpful to read the remainder of the book?

Just note a few rather obvious perspectives: Everything new isn't promising, but almost nothing lasts indefinitely. There are bad trends such as long-term and short-term fuel prices as well as good trends such as the ability to compare opportunities and products online. There are indications that some personal leisure investment and involvement are not only accepted but also applauded in the formerly work-oriented society. Note the way retirees build their timetables and friendships around their leisure lives. My own experience with undergraduates who write scenarios of what they hope their lives will be like suggests that leisure will be quite central to their value and investment systems. On the other hand, economic insecurity can dash many hopes and expectations.

Jumping to Conclusions

Let it suffice to repeat Kahneman's (2011) warning: System 1 decision making can be very costly. System 2 thinking is lazy. It calls for investing time and money in gathering of relevant data, critical analysis, and weighing salience. It's neat and exciting to promote an innovation. It makes us feel advanced and efficacious—we are making a difference. Stressing newness may also be a good marketing theme.

On the other hand, promoting a new opportunity is most likely to be successful when it can be associated with old satisfactions. In Chapter 10 we will examine leisure experience more closely to identify what really turns people on. New possibilities of old meanings would seem to be a good formula.

System 2 thinking is lazy.

In the meantime, in stressing newness, it is important to remember price. It may be true that money cannot buy happiness, but lack of money can rule some attractive opportunities out of consideration. New is good, but there are always limits.

With these warnings, let's move on to identifying potential markets and what is most likely to prompt the investment of those scarce resources: money and time.

4

TARGET MARKETS

Markets are, after all, what it's all about. No market; no business. Most seemingly good ideas do not lead to successful businesses. Again, there is no fixed and clearly identified market for what no one has to do. However, good ideas can not only find but also create markets. For a LB, how?

It's New: Is It a Trend or a Fad?

To begin, there is that "activity life cycle." To repeat, no activity will have sustained growth in participants that just keeps on increasing. However, some will gain a "plateau," usually something below its peak, that provides a basis for profitable business development. Two diagrams follow:

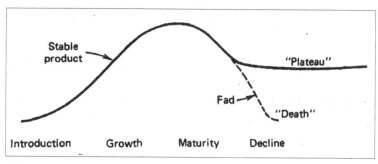

Figure 1. *Product Life Cycle Curves*

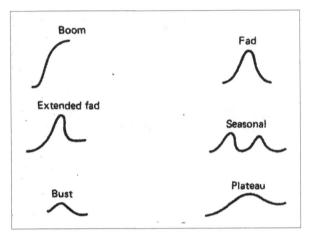

Figure 2. *Product Cycle Curves*

A fad, often referred to in the media as a "craze," gets a lot of attention, has a rapid growth period, and then fades into obscurity. An activity cycle that provides a good market possibility has decline from its growth peak to a sustained plateau level. A common pattern is one that catches investment enthusiasts in overestimating potential markets.

How Can You Distinguish a Viable Trend From a Fad?

To begin with, consider your source. There will always be those with a financial interest in promoting an activity as "the wave of the future." Those who are promoting products, franchises, and consulting are likely to underestimate the potential decline once initial enthusiasm is exhausted. They gain from being unrealistic. At the same time, there are those who are caught up in the activity and sure that everyone will find it as engrossing as they do. For example, recent media attention was given to a new manufactured activity that requires the construction of an expensive set of walls and surfaces, the development of extremely demanding physical skills, and a high injury risk. Furthermore, it would be limited to a young athletic market. Chances for it becoming a good investment? You already know.

Second, there is usually the possibility of parallel innovations. Why *this* game, implement, or venue rather than others competing for the same target market? At this point, all the usual factors of cost, geographical and skill accessibility, and attractiveness come into play. If an innovation is that exciting, it is likely that there will be similar developments, the hula hoop being an exception that tests the rule ... or was it?

Third, be realistic about market segments. In sports, for example, there are large drops in participation in two life-course periods: school-leaving, when opportunities and social rewards fall, and again around age 45, when physical demands may lessen satisfaction and, for some, when family demands compete for time. (This is when softball players become Little League coaches.) We'll examine evaluating target markets further. Here we'll just stop with the warning.

Fourth, and this is VERY BIG, how does the activity fit into current patterns of behavior? For example, videos, DVDs, and now streaming just enlarged and enhanced what most people were doing already. No great change in habits or priorities was required to adopt the new technologies. On the other hand, becoming a private pilot requires great investments of disciplined learning away from home and on other people's schedules as well as thousands of dollars in expense. It should not seem surprising that the numbers of students completing pilot training to even the first-level license is decreasing.

The two repeated rules are important here: Past behavior is the best predictor of future behavior, and look at the baseline numbers. Add to that a close examination of just who the new participants are in age, gender, resources, and culture. Two historical cases may remind us of predictions gone wrong.

Case 1: The Video Game Parlor
If you are old enough, you may remember when new video electronic game parlors sprang up all over the country. Enthusiasts called them a "can't-miss" growth investment opportunity. Those of us who were skeptical saw some simple facts: (a) They required going to an away-from-home site where

access to the game of choice was not assured. (b) Most important, a high proportion of the market was preteen and early teen males who are prone to faddish enthusiasms, have limited spending money, and who get a year older every 12 months. Then, new technologies of at-home games with special boxes and the explosion of home computers made the trip to the emporium unnecessary. At the same time, the major market segment aged, got bored, or moved on, leaving a rather low plateau for the specialized parlor. The limited market segment was easy to recognize. The new competition would have been anticipated by aware "techies."

Case 2: Racquetball

Somewhat further back, there was the "can't-miss" new sport of racquetball. Played first on the often-vacant squash courts on campuses and then growing with dedicated facilities, it seemed an "everyone is doing it" activity to those in the somewhat nearsighted higher education world. Recognizing that those playing as students would need off-campus opportunities when they entered the then-growing economy, clubs were built, especially in urban locales. And for a time, many did well.

The sport was thought to be especially appealing because it was so easy to learn and could be coed. The short-handle racquet made it much easier to hit and control than a tennis or squash racquet. Furthermore, the relatively small court space could offer a winter racquet experience for summer tennis players. However, in a matter of a few years a very high proportion of these clubs had closed or been turned into multiactivity fitness centers. Some entrepreneurs were glad they had not literally set the walls in concrete.

What happened? Paradoxically, the relative ease of gaining beginner skills seemed to work against long-term commitment. As will be analyzed in Chapters 6 and 10, the matching of skill and challenge is central to satisfaction in activity such as sports. If the challenge of the short-handle racquet becomes too low as skill is gained, then the result is boredom. This was one factor in the failure to attract many dedicated tennis players in the winter. The carryover was inadequate. And the market segment was limited by access, cost, work schedules, and competing attractions for too many of those who had left the campus for the world of work.

Foreseeing all this would have required a much more sophisticated analysis than most entrepreneurs would have been capable of doing. Furthermore, estimating how many racquetball players would live or work within a viable distance from the facility would have been quite complex. However, the tale does illustrate just how an adequate analysis would have been multifactorial and interactive.

Question: *Can you analyze a current "craze" from this perspective, preferably your own?*

Hint: Begin with real numbers, costs, and location.

Other Questions

Before leaving this perennial issue for a time, there are a few questions to be put to the activity cycle problem.

- Just how much would most people have to change their habits and life investments to adopt the new possibility?

- Is it possible to estimate from the current growth pattern the potential size of the market for the new experience?

- Are there ways to avoid jumping to conclusions, falling for the halo effect, and being critical of the claims of enthusiasts besides recollecting that the media seek the unusual, not the ordinary?

- Is it possible to distinguish good trends from bad trends? For example, the good trend of increased interest in recreation in natural environments may be countered by the bad trends of increased fuel prices and decreased government investment in resource maintenance.

- Are there underlying trends in discretionary income? For example, if health care costs go up, will leisure spending go down ... and for whom?

Or, whoever said life was simple?

Probabilities and Personal Judgment

Fortunately, we don't have to choose one and ignore the other. A famous Fidelity Funds manager used to recommend that potential investors find stores, services, and products they really liked and then explore investment opportunities. That's good advice for leisure-based investment as well. Especially with franchise development, checking it out, talking to the owner and front-line employees, and watching the clientele can be a really useful first step. But it's only a beginning.

The danger, of course, is that personal enthusiasm and that of those invested may overwhelm System 2 analysis.

The danger, of course, is that personal enthusiasm and that of those invested may overwhelm System 2 analysis.

Question: *Might leisure business investments be especially vulnerable to System 1 decisions?*

Clue: Check the priming effect of first impressions and those newly engaged.

Big Markets: What Most People Do a Lot

Too late! Television retailing is already oversaturated so that profit margins are tiny and competitors are behind every big box storefront and website. The same may be true for other mass-market leisure items. Breaking into the growing mid-market motel business means competing with proven brands with access to capital. I remember talking with the young owner of an attractive motel within sight of a major cross-country interstate who was trying to gain a clientele. The problem was that the chains with their known prices and quality online had most travel units prereserved online before they saw his attractive business.

Are there openings for services in the big-numbers markets, even considering the 80-20 rule? One possibility is location. A careful investigation in convenient locations of camping opportunities, equipment sales and service, specialty guiding and tour arranging (especially in back country), animal care and boarding, or some other facilitation for a large market may reveal an opportunity. However, it begins with knowing the market area numbers, travel patterns, and visitor numbers and goals.

Another possibility is quality. Current providers may have begun with a poor design, have failed to upgrade or maintain, have too many incompetent staff, or have just not understood what the target market really wants in an experience. Some markets invite competition. For example, the beautiful Oregon coast is **Some markets invite competition.** littered with rundown motels and not a few vacant storefronts. Are there openings for upgrading to meet quality expectations? Probably. Or, do higher price developments saturate the upscale market so that renovation or replacement costs would not be return-effective? What about the mid-price "family" market?

A third opportunity is based on new development. A destination natural resource or activity offering may have opened, expanded, or improved its market draw. Such change can also open possibilities for auxiliary businesses. More on public–private synergy later, but it pays to watch what the public-sector agencies are planning and financing. Or not! On the same Oregon coast an attractive private campground met a real market opening when the entrepreneur saw that the public facilities were full and reserved a high percentage of the time. However, clients came for a very special ocean-and-dune experience and demanded quality. Then a secondary business developed in equipment rental.

Some markets are saturated. Reading a list of high-end luxury lodging businesses at burgeoning Park City, Utah, raises the question of how many want to spend $700 to $1,500 a night for a room plus hundreds for a meal. And that doesn't take a snowless December into account. Some product markets are saturated due to the website retailers who now offer "free" (i.e., included in the price) shipping to your door. No checkout lines, parking and traffic issues, or finding items sold out. Unexpected competition can lead to saturation.

> **Clue:** Examine the household composition and trends of your market area. It's free! The U.S. Census breaks down all sorts of population numbers so you can estimate numbers of adult singles, gender, children, income, education, and other target market designations. Big markets may be underserved, especially as populations change.

A study of a changing area in suburban Chicago some years ago revealed two very important factors. First, the population was aging and increasingly single. That is, fewer children and more adults, especially women, were looking for activity outside their apartments. Second, a fairly new freeway cut off easy access to a proposed activity center from a large residential area. Such change both opened and closed markets for relevant activity offerings.

Missing the Target

As just suggested, populations change, both in areas and in larger populations. Such change may create markets previously unidentified. Again, the census figures, especially for urban tracts, can suggest underserved markets. A few commonplace examples follow.

Active Old
The "active old": In the United States people are living longer and in better health. Furthermore, the word is really out that staying active physically, mentally, and socially tends to prolong both health and life satisfaction. Of course, this is

hardly new. I did an analysis of such developing markets for a major consulting firm, Battelle International, decades ago. Retirement villages advertising their range of activities (and downplaying that their residents get older and more infirm eventually) are a multibillion dollar business sector. Nonetheless, recognizing that most older people "retire in place" rather than relocate suggests possible markets for activity as well as services.

> **The proportion of households made up of single adults is rising fast.**

Single Adults

The proportion of households made up of single adults is rising fast. Most are female and employed. Most want to get out of the apartment and be engaged with others who have similar leisure orientations.

Stereotypes

Often stereotypes related to age, cultural background, and even income level prevent the discovery of potential markets. All stereotypes aren't wrong, but many miss the variety of interests within an identified population segment. This raises some doubt about "sophisticated" market segment analysis based on styles (usually labeled with cute acronyms) that may overgeneralize from identifiers such as education level, housing type, neighborhood, and ethnicity.

Niche Markets and Leisure Subcultures

The other end of the big markets, based on what most people do most of the time, are the "niche" markets. They are the .5 of 1% markets in participation. Numbers and trends are difficult to establish because the baselines are so small. Identification of development possibilities is limited by the fact that the activities seldom appear on any of

> **"niche" markets are the .5 of 1% markets in participation.**

the household and census surveys. Nonetheless, quite profitable businesses have been developed by those who know the activity well and can locate in a strategic spot. Now the Internet provides a new means of contacting widely dispersed niche markets. For example, a craftsman who hand built custom bows and arrows in Xenia, Ohio, for decades in a mail-order format with specialty magazine classified ads now could reach a potential world market with a website.

These niche markets have been called "leisure subcultures" in the social science literature. They are formed informally and through narrow-focused organizations based on a specialty activity. Examples are literally endless: from a needlework style to Native American archeology, from rattlesnake hunting to chamber music, from poetry writing to scaling the 12,000-foot mountain peaks. Some are very local. Some bring together those whose residences are widely dispersed. They do, however, have some common characteristics.

- They require a high level of skill development. According to Robert Stebbins' studies of such high commitment "amateurs," their standards are much the same as professionals (Stebbins, 1979).

- They tend to form associations of participants similarly dedicated who become their closest extrafamilial friends.

- They often "play for pay" as semiprofessionals whose major income is from another source.

- They schedule their lives and especially vacations around the activity.

- They are willing to invest disproportionate time and money in instruments, travel, and instruction to hone their skill.

- They attempt to transcend age boundaries for the activity, especially upper age norms.

Stebbins (1979) has studied amateur magicians, chamber music players, baseball players, and several other highly committed devotees of a central life investment. Some can take place almost anywhere. Some require specialized environments—high mountains, white-water rapids, backcountry landing strips, or a core group of theater performers and support workers. A few are high end in expenditures, such as those with rebuilt "war bird" airplanes, and some are very low end, such as hand carvers of folk art objects. Some sing opera, and some pick banjoes. What they have in common is the centrality of the activity to their lives and their willingness to invest in raising their skill level.

> **What they have in common is the centrality of the activity to their lives and their willingness to invest in raising their skill level.**

Some markets rely on location. A set of sheer rock faces 150 miles from an Eastern metropolis can attract enough climbers to support a thriving business that includes supplies, equipment, repair, and instruction. Updrafts off hilly or mountainous slopes can attract enough of those rare birds, soaring pilots.

Other specialty groups can form almost anywhere because the primary requirement is a core base of participants. Woodworking and painting require no special environment, but they do require equipment that can escalate in complexity and costs.

How does one discover such a market? For the most part, since they require a high understanding of the nature and requirements of the base activity, those likely to be successful in a business venture already know about possibilities. Nonetheless, careful analysis is still necessary. A devotion to an activity does not substitute for counting numbers and costs in a System 2 process.

Assessing Target Markets

Any market identification and analysis begins with behaviors. Who, where, when, and with whom are essential questions. One useful way to illustrate this process is to outline an approach to the process. For example, suppose you want to enter what you believe to be a market that is at least stable and could grow in an area with the right new business. Furthermore, you would like to locate in or near the city where you have family and friends. How might you begin?

Locate the Competition

If, for example, your concept is for a fitness center, then first you locate the competition. That would include not only any for-profit enterprises but also opportunities offered by public and not-for-profit organizations such as recreation districts, Ys, churches, synagogues, stakes, and so on, and even neighborhood programs. Locate them carefully on a map of what you believe will be your catchment or market area. Then, begin to explore siting for your enterprise that maximizes access and minimizes competition.

first ... locate the competition.

Do the Numbers

Again, the most recent U.S. Census Bureau tract breakdowns are invaluable. Detailed site analyses are free for the downloading from the feds online. If your business concept is sited and will rely at least in part on retailing, then a full analysis of just who can get to the site and how conveniently is paramount.

Get Participation Data

Match the best participation data with the census demographics. This process is still only preliminary. One problem is that the best numbers on participation are either too general, too old, or too expensive. However, at least it is possible at this point to eliminate gross errors. For example, a proposed bowling center can be evaluated in using the Statistical Abstract trends on participation, estimating a continued decline, taking 25% of the total as the major market, and then looking at population figures for the adjacent census tracts. If it takes, for example, a population of 60,000 within a half hour drive to provide even a minimal base, then many locations are ruled out quickly. Then add in factors such as age and education distributions to further refine the potential market and competitive facilities. If the numbers still hold up, then further investigation may be warranted.

Examine the Competition

A fourth step would be to examine the same style of businesses in similar locations to get a sense of what provisions and styles are successful. For example, with bowling leagues generally losing clientele, are there additional offerings of food and drink, entertainment, meeting space, and programming that offset the losses?

Develop a Business Plan

At this point, the entrepreneur has a wealth of information and needs to go fully into System 2. Just how viable are the target markets, or are System 1 biases blocking critical analysis? It's time to get a full business plan developed and subjected to critical comment by others, including both participants in the activity base and nonparticipants. It is not too early for a "Premortem" (see Chapter 11 for an introduction of this process).

Be Specific

Here the type of business has to be resolved into a particular business in a real location with planned promotion and distribution channels and resulting capitalization requirements. If you are to employ some percentage of OPM (other people's money), remember that your next presentation will be to professional skeptics such as bankers and possible investors. (Again I have a bias from observation; don't bet the homestead, your kid's education, your retirement, or especially the savings of friends and relatives unless they are part of the business. If you can't sell it, take the warning.)

The issue is that everyone does not have the same set of experiences, values, and learning.

Numbers Aren't Everything

There is no substitute for getting the best base statistics possible. However, there is more to identifying target markets. One is much more nebulous but can be critical. You can call it "style" or "culture" or just preferences. The issue is that everyone does not have the same set of experiences, values, and learning. For example, in some cultures, eating together is integral to almost any leisure event. In others, drinking after a sports occasion, doing it or watching, is inseparable from the activity. In some, dancing means that everyone dances, and in others, they watch. What is "classical" in one culture is everyday or even "folk" in another. Styles of engagement may be boisterous and emotional or quiet and contained.

This cultural diversity can make operation of a leisure-based business in locations that draw from several cultures quite complex. Integration may be ideal but makes some clients uncomfortable. A simple example would be a fitness club in which most younger clients prefer mixed-gender settings and socializing, while older clients, especially female, prefer a separated time and place. Or try scheduling a swimming pool for kids, teens, and lap-counting senior fitness swimmers ... not at the same time!

An interesting failure to take culture into account occurred in England over the last decade. An entrepreneur decided to build on the widespread phenomenon of "literary tourism" in that country. Mostly it refers to Joyce walks in Dublin, authors' homes refurnished in period modes and opened to the public, and tours of sites of books and plays by writers from Shakespeare to le Carré. This business concept was based on the work of England's most popular writer of novels, Charles Dickens. It was sited in the heart of Dickens country and called "Dickens World." Great care went into the re-creation of streets, houses, prisons, poor houses, and other artifactual sites. After 10 years, it was evident that the project, although still open and struggling, had failed. No doubt there were many factors, but I would suggest a cultural one. The leisure styles of those who read old novels, however popular, seldom embrace theme parks. In fact, it was literary lovers of Dickens who derided the entire idea.

Cultural elements are also significant for promotion. It's called "market segmentation" in the B school. The elements of an experience that attract one market segment may turn off another. Just look at an urban public beach. Many public recreation managers have had to set up "zones" for different kinds of activity, styles, or cultures. Beach volleyball does not mesh well with preschool children or older adults coming to read.

The point is that a business concept should include the styles of likely use. All those included even in the committed 20–25% of all those who do an activity do not do it alike. As will be suggested further on, one key and often neglected form of market research is observation. Before succumbing to the sales pitch and ordering play equipment for your "keep the kids occupied" play area, go see how kids actually play.

One More Big Clue in Marketing

As will be further analyzed in Chapter 10, a central factor, often *the* factor, in enjoying a recreation experience is other people. What this suggests for the operation of a leisure site will be examined more there. For marketing, there are two major implications.

First, especially for a located business, the most important advertising is free. That is, it is what people tell other people— their family, friends, work associates, neighbors, and so on. Of course, this can work against you as well. Nothing kills a new restaurant quicker than negative personal reviews. The same is true for any business in which you are not selling a Consumer Report-tested product, but an experience. Therefore, Chapter 10 on "Servicing the Experience" may be near the end of the book, but it is first in importance.

Second, Kahneman (2011) analyzes the significance of "associations" in decision making. For marketing, this suggests that promotional programs need to analyze the experiences related to the business and feature them in any advertising or other promotions. It is no accident that advertising for tourist locales usually features attractive people (of all ages up to 70) having fun. The promise of associations is central to choices. (I would add that the common use of celebrities may be the least

A central factor, often *the* factor, in enjoying a recreation experience is other people.

effective advertising device. As a recreational tennis player, I don't identify with the latest 18-year-old power hitter at all. However, if contemplating a vacation with tennis involved, I am very attracted by a program that ensures association with others more like myself.)

Question: *What would be the most important "associational" factors in promoting and managing your business?*

Hint: Go observe multiple sites and times of day.

A Final Note on Bias

In the United States culture and economy, there are a couple of biases that have at least a contextual impact on leisure businesses.

Work Bias

More than in the cultures of most developed economies, work is considered a wonderful thing in the United States, and the very term "leisure" connotes laziness and sloth. In sociology, traditionalists who study work organizations, crime, and even family have generally considered leisure as a topic unworthy of study. For decades, while government research centers in Europe supported social science research into leisure, in the United States use of the dread word guaranteed quick rejection by funding agencies.

More important, cultural values have placed a low value on the area. Recently there has been some change as the importance of the sector in the economy has been recognized by those with money, investment groups, and even bankers. My own research over the years was consistent with studies that found that what is most important to most people and to their life satisfaction is close relationships. Furthermore, immediate communities, including families, find their expression, development, and consolidation to a great extent in leisure activity. Leisure is only slightly connected to work but closely tied to our central associations. More on this later, but note here that evidence is clear that our European colleagues were far ahead of those in the United States in recognizing that leisure is not peripheral.

The bias is receding somewhat. Current emphasis on "successful" aging has directed greater attention to leisure. Literally hundreds of studies have found that when the prerequisites of adequate income and functional health are met, it is regular social, physical, and mental activity that marks those satisfied with later life. Some even call it "leisure" now.

And let me repeat a story from the 4th edition of my text, *Leisure*. Almost 20 years ago, sponsors convened the first major conference on "Work and Family." The research reported on time conflicts and other issues, especially now that the majority of mothers are in the paid workforce, was largely conducted by female scholars. My contribution was a little paper suggesting that there is more to life than work and family and presenting some evidence on the significance of leisure, play, or whatever one prefers to call it. The paper was reprinted in the organization's newsletter where presumably some of the work–family experts read it. Now, years later, the terminology, including conference titles, has changed to "Work and Life." Probably my little counterpoint had little direct influence, but the change is significant.

Capitalist Bias

Critical economist John Kenneth Galbraith pointed out 50 years ago that generally in capitalist economies there is an investment bias. It is simply that a disproportionate share of investment capital goes to the market sector rather than the public sector of schools, health services, national parks and forests, and even the infrastructure that makes most business possible. There is even an ideology that, despite evidence of overbuilding and bankruptcies, the market sector is always more efficient than the public sector. The obvious facts of inefficiencies everywhere and waste and

> ... **generally in capitalist economies there is an investment bias.**

even fraud distributed all over the economy seldom seem to threaten firmly held beliefs.

Not to belabor the argument, there is an important way in which this bias impacts leisure business investment. Just consider the wide range of leisure-based businesses that depend on public programs and resources. Community sports, many arts programs, natural resource-based activity, and school instruction and venues are direct and necessary public provisions. Indirect support is given by highways and other transportation infrastructure, conservation of water and forest resources, safety and law enforcement, and so on. All this takes capital in the form of public investment. (There is no movement to abolish the Coast Guard, only to reduce its funding.) The point is simple: Those making leisure-based investments need to learn to support and work with the public sector.

We'll look at markets and marketing more. However, contexts are important as well.

5

A TIME AND PLACE

There is a long history of references to "leisure time." Traditional economists, firmly believing in the primacy of work, have worked out a number of equations concerning the income–leisure time trade off. Their assumption is that workers usually will choose greater income rather than nonwork time. They see this as (surprise!) a rational decision process in which there is a tipping point at which what money can buy is seen as less valuable than time in which to spend and enjoy it.

Time as a Scarce Resource and Leisure as a Choice

Underlying the trade-off is the premise that there is such a thing as "leisure time" that is left over after work and maintenance tasks are completed. Especially in Europe decades of research have been based on the same concept that there is time free of requirements called in various languages "free time." My argument is that there is no such thing or that it is very rare. Furthermore, the idea can be quite dangerous in developing a leisure-based business.

The counterargument is quite simple. There is seldom, if ever, a time when everything else is completed. For many kinds of employment, operating a business being one, there are always uncompleted tasks. That is why we budget time as well as money. It is a "scarce" resource. One of the great surprises of most new retirees is that "I can't believe how busy I am!" and how many postponed tasks remain undone months and years into retirement. Research shows that time pressures are greatest for employed mothers, especially single mothers of preschool children. Launching—when the last child leaves home—changes but does not obliterate time pressures. You can pretty much figure out differences in time pressures yourself.

The point is that that "free" time is a myth. Leisure is not a leftover but a decision.

The point is that that "free" time is a myth. Leisure is not a leftover but a decision. Engagement in leisure activity requires choosing priorities, allocating time periods, protecting against interference and counterpressures, and persisting in carrying out the choice. Leisure is not a residual quantity of time but an allocation of a scarce resource. Of course, time is more scarce for some than for others.

And there is the counterargument that if time is really scarce and precious, why is so much time spent watching television? There is an answer. Most TV viewing, even some sports for fans, is low demand, low cost, available, habitual, and often erratic in attention. In any case, for a leisure business, marketing is attempting to provoke a choice of the use of scarce resources: time, money, and often energy. The question for the client is not "What do I do with this leftover time?" but "Is this opportunity valued and satisfying enough for the investment of scarce resources?"

This brings us back to the fundamental assumption of leisure marketing and of this book: Selling a leisure experience requires that it promises more satisfaction than alternatives that have lower costs. Again, no one has to do it. It requires that the potential client make time. That is, your business will depend on decisions. They may be System 2 and weigh costs, alternatives,

Again, no one has to do it. It requires that the potential client make time.

and longer term outcomes. Or they may be System 1 in more of a rush to judgment. In any case, they are a choice in a matrix of other possibilities and demands.

Leisure "Takes Place"

With the exception of daydreaming and fantasizing, both significant leisure, leisure has location. It may be conveniently at home, or it may require a costly flight to someplace special. However, residential space and especially privacy are not without cost. Attractive rooms and yards can be quite costly and, therefore, are the result of decisions about resources. "There ain't no free leisure (like lunch)" or, at least, not much.

"Taking place" leads to a number of analytical approaches.

Staying vs. Going

Tourism research has developed and revised the "gravity model" of leisure travel. It was deceptively simple at first. Inertia, staying where you are, is relatively cost free. To get you moving against the pull of gravity requires effort. The further the goal for travel, the greater the energy cost to overcome inertia. Therefore, greater distance requires greater payment in time, effort, and usually money.

> **To get you moving against the pull of gravity requires effort.**

Refinement added that overcoming inertia from a dead stop calls for more energy than keeping moving once in transit. Therefore, the attraction pull of a leisure destination has to be strong enough to overcome initial inertia and then followed by distance costs. For most choices, there is probably also a limit on the distance-time available that rules out certain possibilities.

The implication again is that we are dealing with decisions. The addition is that time-distance adds measurably to the requirement that the anticipated experience be attractive enough to overcome those costs. And the further implication, obviously, is that a leisure opportunity closer to its participant base is likely to do better.

Overcoming Barriers

Second, around most locations are barriers. Mapping "as the crow flies" isn't of much use because we aren't crows. For leisure venues relatively nearby there are issues of public transportation, natural barriers such as rivers, constructed barriers such as freeways, and barriers of perceived danger versus safety, car parking, convenience to customary travel routes, and rush-hour timetables.

Of course, there are money costs related to any business. However, in many cases, the time and travel costs are greater for many potential clients. Credit cards alleviate the pressures of having enough cash on hand. Various payment plans can at least postpone the need for money. But time and distance are always there.

"If you build it, they will come" sounds neat in a movie, but don't count on it. (In fact, it seems that the real "field of dreams" has had an activity life cycle.) If you build it in a location with high travel costs for potential clients, they often won't come, even to an attractive experience.

"If you build it, they will come" sounds neat in a movie, but don't count on it.

"Nearby" to potential clients, as assessed through population analysis, is a complement to any business plan. "On the way" to other destinations is a real convenience. Strip malls are ideal for some retailing and deadly for some activities. The moral is that location is too important to be left to accident or simple availability. It is central to any business strategy.

Money Matters

What can wealth buy? Of course, a lot of things. But in relation to leisure, there is one big one. It is privacy or space. It is well demonstrated that the really wealthy are willing to pay very high prices to avoid most of the rest of us. Private country clubs may have a limited number of memberships costing up to a half million dollars and yearly dues and fees exceeding the average middle-class income. Resorts may be located on islands accessible only by private plane with only a few "cottages" or villas and high levels of service. The theme is privacy and limited access with luxury important but secondary. In Colorado, an exclusive fly-fishing club offers access to fish stocks at uncrowded privately-owned sites...at a significant price.

Luxury and quality of experience are not identical. Furthermore, there are differences in tastes. The once-exclusive and still expensive Rockefeller developments (Rockresorts) were sited in major tracts of space with great natural beauty. Even the name connotes status and privacy. While there have been changes in their policies, they remain places where those who can pay can avoid the crowds for a price. Again, "location, location ... " Privacy alone is not enough. High-end opportunities also have to be designed and operated to offer a great set of experiences. But separated location is the beginning.

Question: *What would be the ideal location for a particular LB? Which compromises are least damaging?*

Clue: Who are the clients and where are they?

Climate Is Also a Choice, Even if Weather Is Uncertain

The climate and weather issue is so obvious that it calls for little explanation. However, that does not make it unimportant.

The attractions are evident. For outdoor sports and activity, participants head south in the winter and north in the summer. For leisure, people escape limiting conditions and seek better environments. This simple fact creates leisure seasons. In turn, those seasons attract residents and visitors. Some leisure seasons are long and some short. Such seasons are a matter of climate, regular changes in weather patterns of temperature, rain and snow fall, sun, and even water fluctuations.

Weather is day to day rather than seasonal. Mean temperatures and average rainfall only suggest probabilities, not what it will be like next week. Forecasts on *weather.gov* are good for a few days ahead but not far enough in advance for most leisure planning involving travel. So there are inevitable disappointments that may not only spoil an experience but also make a return unlikely. Some leisure businesses offer discounts for a return visit or even a raincheck. However, time can't be banked or compensated. If a rafting trip is marred by rain or a ski week by melting snow, some financial adjustment may be possible. But you can't refund time, which is often a more scarce resource than money.

What does this imply for a leisure-based business? To begin with, examine climate conditions very carefully to minimize weather disappointments. Second, be realistic about the season. When climate is combined with school timetables, 3-day weekends, and other general time factors, what looks like several months of outdoor recreation weather may be reduced to a few weeks. Location isn't just place; it is also time.

Government: Partner or Competition?

Overall, federal government spending on recreation provisions is tiny. A Congressional Budget Office estimate of direct federal spending on recreation was .25 of 1% of the total budget. However, that does not include land management and stewardship. When we speak of "natural resource-based recreation," we are usually referring to activity on public land or water. The allocation of resources and management policies and practices are critical for many business plans.

In some cases, government operations compete with the market sector. Federal, state, and sometimes local agencies offer campgrounds, picnic areas, boat launching, ski slopes, and other amenities. In some national parks and recreation areas, government management plans involve leasing facilities to private operators that give a virtual monopoly for on-site lodging, eating, and facility-based activities such as skiing, boating, rafting, and climbing. These leases offer business opportunities but usually require a history of successful operation and adequate

overall the relationship of public sector providers and market-sector businesses is symbiotic rather than competitive.

financial backing. Competing with established franchisees when leases come up for renewal is possible but not simple.

However, overall the relationship of public sector providers and market-sector businesses is symbiotic rather than competitive. Some of the best LB opportunities are located near public sites and provide necessary resources for activity. Examples are too numerous to list. They involve equipment rental and repair, food, lodging, instruction, transportation, and a wide variety of retail goods and services. Of course, the best initial research for such investment possibilities is on-site and compares a number of locations to identify possible new or improved services. Sometimes an entrepreneurial success in one location can be duplicated in another. Often badly managed businesses can be bought or leased and improved.

There are several issues that need to be considered:

- Personal enthusiasm for a site or activity is no substitute for rigorous research and evaluation.

- "The best ones are already taken" does not apply only to the dating and marriage markets.

- The quality of the public resource is crucial and largely out of your control. Plans for future maintenance and development are usually available. Government funding levels, however, may change unpredictably.

- When local cooperation for infrastructure and zoning is required, an assessment of the political climate is basic.

- Symbiosis calls for cooperation, not competition. A good working relationship with the public managers is important. But remember that they have to produce numbers and income like a business in competition for funding. Don't expect them to hand over their best revenue streams.

- Cooperative planning is crucial. Sometimes business owners can be members of a formal planning process. On other issues they can only have input with little influence. But you have to be there!

- Changes in government or management can seriously impact support for particular activities. For example, on a reservoir new rules on powerboats can erode fishing or sailing.

- Governments have long-term investments in the resource that involve traditions if not contracts. However, the more flexibility a business maintains, the less the chance of catastrophic failure. Exit strategies are not a bad idea, even for a new business investment.

- There remains the common bias on the part of many voters that every public program and resource should at least break even and preferably show a profit. The fact is that this may lead to overuse and quality deterioration. Or it may have negative impacts on management that is under pressure to produce short-term results at the cost of long-term resource quality. One important strategy is for the managers of auxiliary businesses to work with and support the public-sector managers when they seek to maintain or improve resource quality. After all, that is the basis of supporting businesses.

One implication of this symbiosis or win–win approach to the public-market relationship is that government is not the enemy. Slogans about "big government" or prejudices against the commonly hardworking and underpaid public employees will poison what needs to be a mutually supportive relationship. Of course, there are mistakes and even sloth in any organization (even universities). But my own experience working with U.S. Forest Service and other public personnel is that they are generally capable and care about the stewardship of the resources they manage. At least, that ought to be the assumption with which business interests begin a relationship.

Question: *How common is government-market cooperation?*

Clue: When is it necessary?

Back to Time: *Carpe Diem* and All That

"Seize the day" is good advice in relation to a LB in several ways.

In assessing investment opportunities, the best chances often are taken by someone else's seizing if one's investors are too slow to come to a decision. Research has demonstrated that alleged experts in stock market investment are unable to "time the market" and that the superior judgment that produces a good yield in one year seldom is repeated the next year. In other words, there is a lot of randomness in the market.

However, in business strategy, there are times that are better than others. A public agency may implement plans to enlarge or improve a resource, creating new business opportunities that are unlikely to be available long. The "activity life cycle" of a new product or activity is only in its initial period of growth for a brief time, and its decline from its peak may come fairly quickly. Getting in and out ought to be more than a matter of luck.

Innovation and promotion, by yourself or others, may open new opportunities. The problem is that no promotion can produce more than a temporary surge in a business with structural limitations. However, there are potential markets out there that can be exploited if the timing is right. As suggested before, distinguishing the "hot new thing" from a promotion-fueled fad requires careful market analysis. On the other hand, those who jumped into handheld electronic game development early are now retiring early and well. Recall that this innovation enhanced what large numbers of people were doing already without requiring radical change in life patterns.

There are potential markets out there that can be exploited if the timing is right.

One other way in which *carpe diem* is relevant to investment is in the decision processes of potential clients. In personal leisure decisions, people not infrequently make snap decisions and jump to an opportunity. As will be analyzed further, reaching the System 1 processes of potential markets can be a very important marketing approach. The "no one has to do it" may switch to "let's do it!" very quickly, especially when there is synergy and support from other people.

More Time Stuff: Timetables and Schedules

As presented before, leisure time is generally not "leftover time." It is chosen, sometimes in a careful budgeting of the hours of a day or the days of a week or month, sometimes in a flash of positive emotion. In any case, time allocated to leisure is chosen rather than residual. It tends to be carved out of the endless possibilities and obligations of life. For example, deciding to play with one person may leave significant others behind and even create later obligations.

For many people, there is no "spare time." As suggested earlier, leisure time is a choice not a residue. Added to this are a number of social changes that impact how and when leisure choices are made.

Women in the Workforce

The big one is the increase of women in the workforce, especially mothers of preschool and school-aged children. The priorities of child care and nurture as well as play have to be organized around work schedules. School hours tend to be fixed. Work timetables are, for most, under the control of others who do not organize them for the benefit of employees. However, such women still desire some time for themselves, even if it is limited. The big change, however, is that the assumption that women were generally available for nonwork activity during the day is blown to pieces. This means that the evening and weekend hours formerly reserved for men now have to be adjusted for employed women as well. Also, leisure opportunities for children can no longer be scheduled with the assumption that mothers can be around-the-clock chauffeurs and organizers.

No More 9 to 5

Along with the employment of women, there is the shift to 24/7 services. The old "standard" workweek is gone for the 80–

90% of workers in services. A further complication is that many service employees in retailing, health care, and other operations do not know more than a week in advance when they will be working. So the assumption that leisure engagements can be scheduled taking a full set of obligations and choices in mind is gone for many adults. Think what this does to the traditional series of events such as instruction in arts, sports, and so on.

The old "standard" workweek is gone for the 80–90% of workers in services.

The 24/7 timetables threaten every traditional assumption about institutional timetables such as church services, school sports, and public events.

Mini-Vacations

One result of such schedule demands is the increased popularity of the "mini-vacation." Three-day weekends or extra days attached to weekends may be reserved for leisure events that require a block of time but no longer the full week. Such mini-breaks are especially attractive for households with more than one employed adult. Synchronizing a 3-day event may be more feasible than an entire week.

The clear implication is that these elements threaten all timetables based on the old workweek and traditional business schedules. Even "banker's hours" have turned into 24/7 operations where competition is severe. For those who would resist such a radical change, the realistic response is "Get over it!"

Some of the problems for a LB are obvious. Regular schedules are problematic, and the size of weekly group activities may be reduced. More women's activities will be in the evening and on weekends, creating space conflicts with what had traditionally been men's preserves. Or women will be shut out of some activities where men express their resentment at losing former privilege.

On the other hand, there are also new opportunities. Clever identification of when and where people are now working may reveal odd hours for activity. Both women and men may engage in leisure before as well as after work, during long lunch breaks as well as weekends, and in flexible rather than fixed times. One problem for the business may be the need to employ staff in such odd hours and have buildings open and ready for 18 rather than 8 hours. The result of seeking extended markets can be increased costs.

Question: *Which changes in social and work timetables inhibit leisure most? Which present opportunities?*

Hint: Household composition is still relevant.

Perennial Questions

Two constant questions are dealt with elsewhere. How to tell trends from fads was introduced in Chapter 4. In Chapter 6, we will address how participants make leisure decisions and how marketing can address the process.

However, there are two other questions related to time and place. The first is "How far and how long?" Analysis of how far potential clients will go for an activity depends on both its attractiveness and whether it is a frequent or occasional engagement. Such analysis has to be specific to the activity, location, and type of target market. The question of duration or how much time a client will invest in an activity also is specific to the nature of the engagement and the composition of the market. A weekly golf game with a regular group may capture a half day of precious time when a gardening project is put off for weeks. Conversely, a commitment to children may outweigh all other possibilities and have scheduling priority.

> **... there are two other questions related to time and place. The first is "How far and how long?"**

Surprisingly, time and distance may be more important than price to many target markets. Cost may rule out some possibilities from consideration but not be of first importance within the range of engagement considered. Personal and relational priorities and commitments are difficult to assess but are often most salient to leisure choices. More on this in the next chapter.

Then add to these complications the fact that competition is everywhere. "Big box" and "little box"—no market goes unmet for long. On to decision making!

6

MAKING LEISURE DECISIONS

Marketing for a leisure-based business is more than product promotion. Compare the process with selling a car or kitchen appliance.

With the car or range, there is necessity. Some purchases are upgrades, but there is usually push as well as pull. Something is unsatisfactory about the current item, from full failure to stylistic dissatisfaction. Supporting your promotion is some national advertising. Often underlying the decision will be ratings of quality from consumer organizations. A System 2 decision then takes into account competition from other dealers and other brands. While some sales are engineered once the consumer is on the lot or in the store and impulse decisions are not unknown, for the most part the competition, now augmented by all sorts of websites, is fully known to the seller and buyer.

With a leisure purchase, there is no necessity.

With a leisure purchase, there is no necessity. Remember Rule 1. Generally there is no national advertising base. Competition is most often a different activity unknown to the seller, or doing nothing special at all. Decisions, with a lack of evaluative information, often resemble System 1 more than System 2. And, most important, you are selling an experience, not products that can be at least mentally placed side by side and subjected to a cost-benefit analysis. Even a travel package with lots of competition may boil down to an "I've always wanted to see ..." rather than an online comparison of hotel amenities. In brief, the anticipated experience has to have its own appeal; the big question is "How do you enhance the appeal?"

Which System ... or Both?

According to Kahneman (2011), System 1 is largely pre-analytical, even impulsive. It consists of a set of prejudgment elements and associations. In a sense, the decision process itself is prerational and emotional. System 2 weighs alternatives, assesses what is known and unknown, and analyzes even the process as well as the decision.

It would be tempting to declare all leisure choices as System 1 and then base marketing on evoking positive emotions in relation to the anticipated experience. Then all the marketing that is primarily analytical, comparative, and based on cost-benefit analysis would be ruled out. That would, of course, be hasty and shortsighted. For example, when deciding whether to fly or drive to a vacation destination, most of us do compare price as well as convenience, recollections of previous good and bad experiences (e.g., the airport), and time costs. In selecting which golf course to play, price versus crowding on weekends is usually figured in.

So, elements of both decision systems need to be considered in marketing. The system "types" are, after all, heuristic devices to aid analysis, not either/or real-life descriptions. However, given that, in what follows we will tend to emphasize System 1 elements just because they tend to be overlooked in most conventional economic models and approaches.

The basic principle, then, is that in a LB, we are selling the experience. There are many secondary or contributive factors such as environment, equipment, learning process, personal relationships, and so on. But basic, especially to promotion, is bringing to the client's attention some associations or recollections of a positive experience. Ideally, the images are of a "peak" experience that makes costs worthwhile or even causes them to be forgotten.

In Chapters 7 and 10, we will go deeper into the elements of leisure experience and what tends to create "highs." At this point, we will focus on two themes.

The First Factor in Satisfaction: Other People

Different approaches to identifying the elements that contribute most to a good experience almost all come out with the same result: other people. Setting aside for the moment solitary activity, what makes or breaks most experiences is whom we are with. Often those companions are our primary relations from family, household, or other central relationships. Conversely, being with the wrong people can ruin even a rafting trip through the Grand Canyon.

. . . .what makes or breaks most experiences is whom we are with.

Highest happiness tends to come from doing something we like with the people most important to us. In other situations, engaging new relationships with people we find interesting and attractive can also yield high levels of positive feelings. Some relationships are reliable and comfortable and others new and exciting. However, in general, the people come first. It is usually not difficult to recall events in which some activity or place we enjoy was spoiled by other people.

As a result, marketing quite rightly is generally most effective when the experience we are selling is associated with people we want to be with. Back when it was assumed that travel markets were dominated by the relatively young, there were all the "sand, sun, and sex" illustrations designed to lure that target market. Now that more mature markets such as post-parental adults and the active old are emphasized, the photo strategy becomes a bit trickier. However, other people are still central.

The main implication is quite clear. Once target markets are identified for whatever your business is selling, advertising and other promotion should highlight the other people they are most likely to want to be with. It may be couple oriented, same or other sex singles, children who can play with children, or intellectually stimulating oldsters. All these associations and others are central to selling the experience. And, as will be stressed in Chapter 10, they are also central to management and operation of the business.

System 1 Marketing

The aim will be to associate your offering with symbols that evoke memories or aspirations of positive experiences. The strategy involves analyzing the primary elements of the experience and selecting symbols—visual, verbal, or combinations—that are likely to prompt positive memories or anticipations. It can be quite different from a rational cost-benefit analysis. It is likely to involve images more than ideas. The strategy is to put these associations foremost and cost-benefit calculations in the background.

[System 1 marketing] is likely to involve images more than ideas.

As will be analyzed further, there is more to such associations than just feelings of pleasure. Nonetheless, it is images, symbols, and other recall "hooks" that come first. Of course, attractive environments are important. So are suggestions of doing the activity, whether surfing, hiking, or listening to great music. The intention of the promotion is to guide positive associations. Then when the decision process moves on and may include System 2 elements, the "halo effect" puts them in a positive light. The evoked set of images or emotions will frame the choices.

> **Question:** *Develop a website (or ad) that uses this approach to support a positive decision for your actual or proposed leisure business.*

> **Clue:** Think about your own peak experiences with the activity or resource.

System 2 Marketing

This emphasis on evoking positive associations does not mean that the traditional System 2 factors are irrelevant. In fact, for repeat business, crucial to most leisure businesses, they are all part of the total experience.

Of course, price and place are important. Other than the easy part of pricing, researching the pricing policies of successful similar businesses and any that might be competition, there are a few clues:

- Begin by analyzing the target markets and their likely financial condition. In some areas, a low initial price may be necessary to get clients started.

- In the same way, make no assumptions about household composition. Too many businesses still emphasize "family" rates rather than dealing with the variety.

- Analyze the participation styles so that pricing can meet variations in regularity, peak hour use, and group composition.

The point is simply that pricing is one integral element of the total attraction package. It may not make potential clients want to do it, but failure to recognize real life and financial conditions can keep people away.

The place issue has already been addressed. Access to a sited business can make the difference between regular use and occasional patterns that deteriorate into disappearance. The service provided and its scheduling may determine how important location may be. What is critical is a strategy that begins by understanding that for even the 20–25% who do an activity regularly there are always alternatives. Just being the nearest opportunity doesn't cut it.

Just being the nearest opportunity doesn't cut it.

Other elements in the experience will be addressed later. The overriding issue is that *every* aspect of the business strategy should be "enabling." Anything that rules out any segment of target markets should be alleviated if it cannot be eliminated.

Marketing to Real Decisions

Not to overstress business school omissions, but there are two sources of inadequacy: the assumption of rational or "reasoned" choices and a lack of understanding of the special qualities of a leisure-based business. To be fair (somewhat), the reasoned choice models can become quite successful in prediction. They are, of course, probabilistic. That is, they predict likelihood of certain outcomes given a set of preconditions. For marketing purposes, there are two problems. First, they don't predict for any individual, only for probability within a given set. Second, very seldom do we know, when devising a marketing strategy, that much about prospective clients. One reasoned choice model (developed by two colleagues) presupposes knowing so much that it becomes generally unusable. My exaggerated metaphor is that it has a subject with one foot already over the cliff and leaning toward the abyss. Guess what; it predicts close to 90%.

In this section, it is the decision process to which we are giving attention. Again, a different model or models seem more useful. The first takes into account prerational responses rather than systematic definitions of the situation. Association and emotional "halos" often count for more in leisure decisions than weighing outcomes, alternatives, and costs. According to Kahneman's (2011) Prospect Theory there are other elements. Highly significant is "risk aversion." Decisions seem to give greater weight to avoiding loss than reaching goals. For leisure, this suggests that promotions that call up possible threats may turn away clients even when a rational assessment would suggest that the likely outcomes are worth the risk. For example, fear of failing to find acceptance in a group of strangers may keep clients away.

It also suggests that the "risk versus comfort level" of a possible experience—in social acceptance, skills required, or evaluative observation by others—may rule out the activity itself.

The trick seems to be to associate the contemplated experience with positive symbols and use promotion that does not unintentionally elicit common threats. For example, in sports or the arts, using "stars" to illustrate the activity may actually turn away the risk averse. I have had a running argument with sports gerontologists who persist in telling about the exceptional swimmers or runners who are world class at age 85 rather than more ordinary folk who stay active with attainable levels of performance. We do know that familiarity reduces the perceived threat of almost anything. (I have flown professional "smoke jumpers" who were as apprehensive about my off-airport landings as I am about jumping out of an airplane.) As will be elaborated further, in marketing we want to associate the "experience value" of what we are selling with what minimizes social or competence threats.

Question: *Can you describe a picture of high moments of your favorite activity?*

Hint: The content may be more than emotional.

Implications for Promotion and Marketing

- **This is not a program.** Leisure businesses are too varied for that. But some hints and clues can be useful as discussed below.

- **The first is to identify the "peak experiences" related to the activity and setting.** One simple way is to ask current participants what they remember as most enjoyable from previous events. There is also some quite pointed research on the subject (Chapters 10 and 11). It is the peaks that tend to draw clients back and the valleys that turn them off.

- **The two foci are simply what people do and whom they are with.** The action component may be multifaceted. However, the core is the part of the total experience in which players are most fully engaged.

- **The community–intimacy factor may vary for even the same client.** While most of those in consistent primary relationships—family, lovers, close friends—find the highest satisfaction over time in those ties, there may be singular events in which some element of novelty becomes salient. For example, bars and clubs in which the "fancy milling" is designed to explore new relationships may feature novelty. The same theme may seem rather unexciting, but it still important for older persons who have lost primary companions. Sorry if this is belaboring the "other people" theme, but it is too often neglected in business schemes and management.

- **Very important to persons of all ages is the "competence theme."** Opportunities to demonstrate ability are central to so many leisure experiences. What may be surprising is that this element of satisfaction does not seem to lessen with age. It is obvious for the striving and developing youth. However, perhaps because of questions raised by aging, it is also central for older women and men as they seek to maintain and even strengthen their sense of competent selfhood.

There are other clues related to System 1 marketing. One is familiarity. Just the opposite of challenge, returning to places and people that have produced good experiences in the past is also a recurrent motif. Most people don't want to be challenged or seek novelty all the time. However, in marketing this element may need relatively little attention.

There is a kind of bipolar scheme underlying some leisure marketing.

There is a kind of bipolar scheme underlying some leisure marketing. At the one end are the experiential highs, both of engagement and relationships. At the other end is inertia. Inertia is the extreme of the "No one has to do it" factor. For LB marketing, inertia in all its forms is the enemy. If we include the now omnipresent home and portable games and entertainment within the inertia spectrum, then inertia may be the big foe.

How can this inertia be overcome in marketing? We will examine the nature of leisure experiences further to begin to find answers.

7

WHAT DOESN'T CHANGE ... MUCH

When one has been doing and interpreting research in a field for over 40 years, there is the danger of becoming embedded in old models and approaches. Being a scientist, including a social scientist, means to never stop learning because current knowledge is always partial and subject to revision. Some of the perspectives employed in this book are quite recent; others are quite old. In this chapter, the premise is that the age of a model or theme neither validates nor invalidates it. Also, the "latest thing" may be just another fad.

The next few pages will focus on some explanatory approaches that have been around for some time, even decades. That does not make them "eternal truths" to be worshiped as iconic and immutable, nor does it make them outmoded and useless. In fact, some are extremely valuable in assessing markets and strategies for leisure businesses.

Social Contexts

Sartre did a disturbing little play in which the theme was that "hell is other people." (Are there any people with whom you would want to be enclosed in a room forever?) In any given context, that may be true in this life as well. A small group tour in a van or yacht accompanied by two or three really unpleasant people can be a disaster. However, most often we seek leisure settings and activities where we will be with people we value and enjoy. In fact, in urban areas (where most people live), we are most likely to make friends in leisure engagement rather than work, especially if that includes children's play programs and religious organizations.

Kahneman (2011, p. 395) reports one of countless studies that finds that given reasonable health and a measure of economic security, the major factor in life satisfaction is regular interaction with people we enjoy and care for. That primary group may change as we move through the life course, but having contact with friends and loved ones remains central to a "good day."

The Life Course and Predictable Changes

Social psychologists tend to use the term "life span," but that label overemphasizes chronological age. Family sociologists used to refer to the "family life cycle," but that makes it seem too regular and predictable. "Life course" suggests that there is a progression related to common transitions but that each journey is unique and subject to unpredictable changes. (For a fuller account of this approach in relation to leisure, see my text, *Leisure*, 4th edition, 2012, or even earlier editions.)

The theme is that there are sequences of changes in social contexts up to the end of any life journey.

The theme is that there are sequences of changes in social contexts up to the end of any life journey. These changes, whether sudden or predictable transitions, have impacts on leisure interests, companions, resources, and orientations. First, however, a warning: Few people make the normative journey all the way without disruptions. More choose or are forced into variations. For example, over half of the children in this country will experience some period without a pair of parents in their home. And, so evident at this time, the predictable work "career" has become a series of jobs for most adults.

Beginning with school years, the traditional life course goes something like this:

- Preparation: education and other "getting ready" settings
  - Seeking to establish a new household
  - Entering the world of work, hopefully one with a future

- Establishment:
  - Early: seeking regularity in primary relationships and work
  - Middle: consolidating home and work including marriage and children for most
  - Late: launching children (hopefully) and settling for a position in a work trajectory

- Consolidation and Acceptance:
  - Preretirement and accepting who and where one is
  - Retirement and aging, reestablishment without work structure
  - Reinvestment despite limited future
  - Frailty and death

This roughly is the predictable pattern. Some of the transitions have great impacts on leisure meanings, contexts, and resources. Leaving school and the parental household is obvious. Becoming a parent seems to cause greater change than marriage itself. Late midlife with its recognition that the end is nearer than the beginning and that prospects are limited can turn work limits into leisure investments. Retirement, of course, transforms timetables and obligations as well as income for most. Frailty, at an age no one can predict, closes off many leisure experiences.

And there are the traumatic events. Divorce or death end what is for most the primary relationship and may come at any age. Loss of employment impacts every aspect of life, especially economic security. One study I directed in Peoria, Illinois (Kelly, 1987), examined transitions in the life course focusing on age 40 and older. Not surprisingly, most individuals had at least one major and unpredictable life-changing event. And most had found resources within themselves or with others to come through the trauma and rebuild life. Furthermore, for those coping with change, leisure investments were an important positive factor.

Some important perspectives relevant here for leisure marketing and management are discussed next.

- Identifying where your clients are in the life course gives critical information about their goals, obligations, schedules, resources, and associations. For example, cultivating a daytime market of preschool parents has usually meant offering some means of child care. Now, however, those parents are usually in the workforce so that time is the scarce factor and flexibility crucial. On the other hand, retirees have flexibility but often seek social contexts to replace work. And, to be realistic, some life course periods pretty much rule out leisure that is costly in time as well as finances.

- The big change is that a predictable life course with regular periods and "passages" is now very much a minority pattern. Furthermore, leisure engagements may serve to aid transitions and especially offer social contexts for those who have to rebuild. The explosion of online "matching" services suggests that some leisure programs may be missing a vital opportunity. This is more than "singles bars" and "love cruises." It is in the ordinary round of life that we are mostly likely to meet and engage compatible others. With all the problems of work relationships, that leaves leisure.

> ... leisure engagements may serve to aid transitions and especially offer social contexts for those who have to rebuild.

- A gradual shift in sexual norms has already had impacts with many of the implications yet to be understood. A generation, and certainly two, ago seeking sexual access led many into marriage. Now sexual access is more widely available and accepted as a new norm by large segments of the population. The changes include both genders, all education levels, most ethnic identifications, and even ages flirting with legal limits. Furthermore, with numbers skewed toward lower education levels, about half of all babies are born to unmarried mothers. Consider what this does to the former family life cycle with predictable periods and transitions. Also think about how the greater openness to intimate sexual activity, a trend that began over a century ago, has transformed the expectations and behaviors in and around many leisure settings. How a business can respond to such changes will have to be worked out in the local situation, perhaps differentiating the urban scene from the family-oriented suburb. In any case, the frequency with which "meeting" leads to something more transforms the sexual dimensions of many leisure settings.

The new majority is those in transition. Jobs, families, locales, and even values change. We learn and, hopefully, grow through the life journey. As work seems more and more limited for most adults and traditional institutions lose appeal, there we are: the multipurpose LB.

Question: *Which life changes may create a greater openness to new leisure investments?*

Clue: Do they involve time and timetables?

How Can a LB Respond to Fluidity?

One constant element of leisure is change. That is, there seems an almost inevitable mixture of commitment to activities that we find especially satisfying and those that we like to explore. Both are significant as the life journey is characterized by change as well as predictability. The challenge of something new is contrasted with the comfort of something familiar. Just in terms of numbers, the market for familiarity is probably the greater. The central market for an activity opportunity is usually those who would like to do it more or in an improved setting.

Targeting markets may begin with the population and participation numbers, but it does not end there. There is more than one pathway to leisure engagement, from doing something familiar with friends to taking the risk of something new with strangers. Marketing can address both, but not necessarily in the same style or medium. Management can be sensitive to the needs of both, if not necessarily simultaneously. (I can't count the number of tennis facilities that don't seem to respond to visitors who don't know anyone and are not there for a week-long "clinic.")

Other Limits: Economic and Cultural

In assessing markets there is a seeming dilemma. For at least two decades, the purchasing power of most of the population has declined. Those with substantial investments have ample discretionary income. Those highly educated and/or skilled also have discretionary income for leisure but often are under heavy time pressures. The "middle mass" who are employed have on average diminished income to spend on leisure. Then, the 40% of poor or "near poor" are, of course, quite restricted in nonessential spending.

On the other hand, in many locations it is that middle mass, the 45–60%, who are underserved.

The dilemma is simply this: Leisure provisions for the upper 5–15% are most likely to be priced for an adequate profit. This is hardly a secret. Therefore, market sector leisure provisions are heavily skewed toward that market sector. The result? Competition. That is the favored target market for any provision that is costly.

On the other hand, in many locations it is that middle mass, the 45–60%, who are underserved. A business plan that can reach that market and still make a profit may beat the failure odds. But how? One strategy is to piggyback on public facilities and environments to minimize investment and maximize the potential market.

A second strategy is to offer services such as summer wilderness hiking, water sport instruction, reasonable rental opportunities, and hunting and fishing guiding rather than facilities.

Clues to such strategies? Location, experience with the activity base, flexibility, part-time employees such as students, and a host of other ways of limiting initial investment and operating costs.

There are also cultural limits on what clients are willing to attempt and to pay for. For example, Hispanic families seem less likely to divide up for leisure than Anglo units. In some cultures there remain different definitions of what is appropriate for young women than for young men. Sports take a higher place than the arts in some cultures. Styles of music that attract some groups repel others.

There are cultural changes. However, we are not "plastic personalities" who can readily adjust to almost any situation. Many of the persistent cultural themes are related to gender. Others have to do with what people wear, the composition of vocabularies, and specific contextual behaviors. One clue to sensitive understanding of cultural elements in a leisure business is to get out from behind the desk and closely observe what is really going on. Ms. or Mr. Entrepreneur, everyone is not just like you.

And Everything Doesn't Work

There is no substitute for constant and systematic evaluation. Your business school will, quite appropriately, demonstrate how good accounting practices can be central to monitoring a business and identifying what is not working. A spreadsheet that allocates income and expenditures by the various sectors of a business and even by market sectors can identify many errors in operation as well as what might best be expanded.

However, to repeat, there is no substitute for getting out there and observing. Numbers are relatively easy. Mapping spatial use and adding up time uses need not require a computer. Analysis will often identify space that is not being used and space that is crowded, time spent in conversation in and around an activity rather than in direct play, groupings who do or do not participate together, and secondary activity that is part of the experience but does not require dedicated and designed space. Traffic patterns are important. Gathering points, often not designed for socializing at all, may lead to more efficient design and enjoyable experiences.

But the manager has to be willing to be wrong! If concepts, designs, and operational styles are to be defended rather than evaluated, then the business is headed for trouble. New clients, who are highly desired, may bring with them different styles of both play and socializing.

What Is *the* Leisure Experience ... If Any?

Various scholars and self-ordained "philosophers" have written about "the leisure experience." The mere fact that they do not all designate the same experience suggests the topic may be more complicated. Contemporary designs intended to produce positive outcomes self-evidently are more complex than focused on a single theme. For example, the constantly changing and developing epitome of leisure business, Walt Disney World, has excitement and relaxation, challenge and comfort, high technology and simple themes, education and entertainment. There seems an infinite variety of things for sale, many themed to match the exhibits and rides. Shows, rides, 3-D multiscreens and surround sound, and so on are aimed at a range of ages and groupings. If any elements are consistent, they are high quality and high cost.

> **... experiences are multidimensional.**

The point is that leisure experience is embedded in the activity and the environment. The core experiences of the arts vary for performance and appreciation. Engagement in competitive sport is certainly different from being a spectator. White-water kayaking and beach sunning both involve water but in quite different ways.

Furthermore, experiences are multidimensional. Is there, for example, a "wilderness experience"? If you read the literature of various conservation organizations, you might believe in such a global concept. Counter to this, a social psychologist, B. L. Driver, doing research for the U.S. Forest Service, has explored reported backcountry experiences and found a rather complex scheme. My summary of the results (Kelly, 2012, p. 290) includes the following schema:

1. **Social:** social recognition, family togetherness, being with friends, meeting new people, exercising leadership, and sharing skills.

2. **Personal expression and development:** achievement, reinforcing self-image, competition/testing, discovering and learning in reflection and physical fitness.

3. **Experimental (intrinsic):** stimulation, risk-taking, tranquility, using equipment, and nostalgia.

4. **Nature appreciation:** enjoyment of scenery, closeness to nature, learning, open space, and privacy.

5. **Change:** rest, escape from pressure and routines, avoiding crowds, and getting away from problems.

Note not only the variety but also the seeming contradictions. And this is only one type of leisure environment and related set of activities. It does not represent basketball, distance running, painting, dancing, or a hundred other activities. How is it possible to design and program for such variety?

First, personal experience with the activity base of a LB is essential. Along with personal experience, listening to and observing others in the same environment will add to your analysis. And, with a clue from Driver's results, recognize that everyone in a leisure environment or activity may not gain the same outcomes and satisfactions. For example, a retiree at the tennis center may seek challenge and involvement, while a stressed, employed mother may hope for separation and relaxation. And both may be experienced in the same setting and in different styles of engagement in the same activity. To add to the complexity, think about the multiple experience dimensions of travel; a night club with drinking, eating, dancing, and entertainment; or a workshop in ceramics design.

Second, one clue to sorting out the experiences is to identify "peak" experiences in an activity or involvement sequence. What are the elements that are, if not unique, at least special to an activity and setting? And are the peak experiences the same for every participant in a particular event or activity? However, it is most often the peaks that draw a client back to the business. And peaks are especially crucial to marketing and management if target markets are to be attracted and nurtured.

> **... one clue to sorting out the experiences is to identify "peak" experiences.**

Question: *Can you identify your own peak experiences?*

Hint: They may change.

Peak Experiences: Flow and Skill

Two lines of research point to central dimensions of peak experiences. Significantly, it is those who experience such highs who are most likely to be regular participants, invest time and money, and become the core of the market spectrum for any particular activity or setting.

Flow: The Meeting of Skill and Challenge

Mihaly Csikszentmihalyi (1976) is an innovative research psychologist whose adoption of the concept of "flow" has received wide attention in a variety of quarters. The basis is rather simple: People in flow experience a condition in which they become so absorbed in an activity that they lose consciousness of time and place, of anything other than deep involvement in the action. This state occurs when there is a meeting of challenge and skill or competence. When skill is greater than the challenge, the result is boredom. When the challenge is too great for the skill, the result is anxiety. Satisfaction, then, results in some middle range of a viable skill/challenge situation.

His research approach has been based on "experience sampling" in which at a random time, an attention-getting signal calls a person to pause and record what he is doing, where, with whom, mood, and level of satisfaction and involvement. Across all age ranges and in a variety of activities, flow, satisfaction, and positive mood are highest in that skill/challenge concurrence. Obvious settings for identifying flow include sports, creative arts, learning difficult skills, and other involving activities. He and his colleagues also confirm the general finding that involvement in communication with valued associates including intimacy may produce a similar high. (I have suggested an extension of the concept to the correlate of "social flow.")

Implications for a LB are self-evident. Any design or management that can increase the likelihood of skill/challenge involvement is most likely to produce the kind of experiences that will create return business and that most effective advertising, word of mouth. How flow can be supported and enhanced in any setting depends on a number of social and environmental factors that vary with the activity. However, the peaks of flow may be the most consistent experiences in attractive leisure offerings.

> **... the peaks of flow may be the most consistent experiences in attractive leisure offerings.**

Amateurs: The Dedicated Core

Robert Stebbins (1979) developed the concept of "amateurs" out of his own experience as a nonprofessional chamber music player. He has since investigated a wide range of activities: magic, baseball, archeology, theater, and others. His findings are a correlate to Csikszentmihalyi's. The amateur does not depend on the activity for her/his primary income. It is, however, central to the amateur's personal and social identity, investment of time and money, primary relationships, and life satisfaction. In some cases, as with musicians and (in the old days) baseball players, there may be some pay per performance to create "semipros." In the arts of painting, ceramics, writing, and others, those most adept may insist on selling their creations as a validation, even though the income may not be central to household finances. As with flow, the skill/challenge is central. And, according to Stebbins, the standards of performance are much the same as for professionals.

Such amateurs can be the core of a stable market . . .

Such amateurs can be the core of a stable market for many businesses. Furthermore, their performances may attract others to the activity. In some situations, they may be part-time instructors in required skills. And their enthusiasm for the activity, especially when it is immediate in contrast to televised professionals, may be a major form of unpaid promotion for a business.

The central dimensions in flow and for amateurs are constant skill development, challenging settings and materials, regular association with other amateurs seeking flow, and access to opportunities that are feasible and affordable.

Question: *How can you apply these two themes to your leisure business plan or hope?*

Clue: Both flow and amateurism involve skill development and other people.

An Often Overlooked Question: What Do People Actually Do?

Don't we know what people are doing at their kid's ball game, on the beach, while hiking, and so on? A few, not very many, studies have offered some surprises and raised some interesting issues for a leisure-based business. The main contribution of trying to answer this question is to challenge clichés that may mislead the leisure entrepreneur.

To begin with, there is golf. A common assumption is that the particular challenges of the sport and the attractions of the outdoor environment compose the activity called "golf." However, take a walk around the course and clubhouse to see what else is going on: conversations, arguments, eating and drinking, waiting, keeping score, and a variety of emotional expressions. Over the hours in an event called "golf" there is a lot going on, some enjoyable and some not. There are reasons why golf has been called "a good walk spoiled." However, not playing golf misses the peaks of flow and the satisfactions of skill demonstration and improvement.

Don't we know what people are doing . . . ?

An observational study at Corps of Engineers reservoir beaches in the Pacific Northwest came up with the surprising finding that people spend far less than half their time swimming, boating, and playing beach sports. Rather, most people most of the time were talking, resting, reading, drinking, flirting, exhibiting themselves in various ways, and staying out of the water.

What do people actually do when they are at a tourism destination? Of course, the variety of activity is great. However, for many tourists, the most time-consuming activities are shopping, eating and drinking, and resting.

What is the most common away-from-home leisure locale for Americans, and many others? It is clearly the shopping center, especially when the satisfaction of "doing something" can be gained by purchasing stuff. "Things," often inexpensive, are symbols of efficacy for many without any serious demands on skill. It is not just teens who hang out in the mall. Various attempts to incorporate recreational opportunities within the megamall have met with mixed results. They have the advantage of being where people are. How many cope with the crowds, parking, and other barriers consistently has proven problematic. Also, the wide mix of patrons in a mall has limited some activities.

Finally, where does fantasy fit in? The leisure of the mind and imagination, often melding into dreaming, is common for almost everyone. Students of the mind have demonstrated that imaginative activity has many developmental and therapeutic values. For many, the fantasy is connected to real activity. (When I was a teen ball player, I used to pitch entire White Sox games in my semi-wakeful fantasy mind.) To my knowledge, no one has done convincing research connecting fantasy to actual leisure choices and satisfactions, but I am rather sure that the relationship is there. It may even lead to decisions, activity, and time–money investments.

Leisure Investment Issues

The overall theme of this chapter has been relative consistencies in leisure behavior, motivations, satisfactions, and choices. This theme has been related to marketing in some examples and questions.

The first issue revolves around central and consistent satisfactions. Communities formed around commitment to a common activity, self-identification based on a skilled activity, and peaks of skill development and exercise (flow) are and are likely to remain central to a leisure experience that people find attractive and want to repeat.

The second consistent theme has more to do with resources, conflicts, and regular associations. The life course is one useful approach for market analysis and targeting. The greater and greater number of deviations from that model and market segments in transition at any time in life's journey also offer attractive marketing opportunities.

It is possible to argue that the needs for close and consistent relationships, for gaining and demonstrating competence, and for satisfying self-definitions are found more often in leisure than in work in contemporary society. In any case, leisure is not peripheral, leftover, or trivial to a very large number of people. And they are the leisure markets.

There is a wide variety of leisure business opportunities. Some are large and some small. Even though most entrepreneurs do not begin by envisioning "big business," that dimension is a part of the scene that any business concept must take into account.

8

THE BIG PICTURE

Most businesses start out small. However, the business environment includes some VERY BIG businesses. They are quite different in many ways from small start-up operations. However, they are relevant in at least three ways:

- They are a part of the "experience economy."

- They may provide business training for those new to the field. (However, for the most part they train people for their own business and pay low hourly rates.) The huge scale of many businesses, especially in tourism and community development makes them the largest source of employment in many fields. The problem, of course, is that entry-level jobs tend to be poorly paid and competition for advancement is keen.

- Perhaps surprisingly, they may be competition for small experience businesses.

What Is the "Experience Economy"?

To begin with, some leisure-based businesses are really big. Examples include the Disney enterprises, Las Vegas, Netflix, hotel chains, and restaurant franchises. Size does not always mean quality. However, such businesses have had opportunities to try out different styles, promotions, management approaches, and personnel. They can afford a few mistakes because their size can absorb occasional losses. Usually, they have access to capital, either from their own income or through established credit arrangements.

Anyone in the field can learn from them. However, this does not mean that they do everything right. Big organizations often become resistant to change. As turning a big ship takes time and space, so real shifts for a big corporation meet resistance, usually from those who have seen success in the past from what they have developed. In fact, one fun exercise is to visit Disney World, a theme park, or a megaresort with a critical eye to look for practices that seem to block or erode experiences.

The designers of a leisure-based site should keep the hoped-for experience of clients central.

On the other hand, many businesses are sensitive to threats. For example, some theme parks, including Disney, have heard critics deride their "fakery" and now seek to design and promote authenticity. Contradictions of designing and producing authenticity would seem to present some difficulties. Nonetheless, a fake English pub at Disney World avoids the problems of fighting one's way to the bar for a pint as well as getting to the real thing. There is the old adage: If it isn't authentic, fake it!

What is central, however, is that bigness does not preclude the issue of personal experience. An architect may design an office building to make an exterior statement, even at the cost of interior efficiency. The designers of a leisure-based site should keep the hoped-for experience of clients central. It would be possible to argue that part of the genius of the Disney designers in California is just this priority. Certainly Walt himself set out with the family experience in mind when he took the great leap from animated films to the pioneer Disneyland.

One Approach: Business as Theater

The metaphor of "business as theater" is borrowed from a book by Pine and Gilmore (1999). They argue that more and more businesses are marketing an experience rather than a fixed product. Furthermore, the experience is largely leisure based. However, leisure experience is more than entertainment. It involves eliciting a response from the clients who become involved in the total experience.

Without getting too deeply into the "dramaturgical" background of this approach, the theater metaphor is very suggestive. It suggests that a leisure business does more than provide a service. Rather, the outcome involves reciprocity between the provider and the client. Even big leisure businesses focus on the individual and small-group experience. Big markets call for customization more than a mass phenomenon. (You might do a critique of much of the Las Vegas style from this standpoint.) In fact, the aim becomes experience that involves the client. Pine and Gilmore (1999) call this "transformation."

> ... good theater is designed to produce that involvement, not just to "put on a play."

That is, something occurs in the encounter between the provision and the participant. While their examples of fitness and religion seem a bit weak, the idea that something happens to the participant is on target. The experience may be intense and involving (flow), or it may be more diffuse as a form of entertainment. In any case, as in theater, there is reciprocity between the stage and the audience. And, good theater is designed to produce that involvement, not just to "put on a play."

Again, the aim is the experience, usually a process with highs and lows. The business offers an environment, a setting, a design, a process, or a "play," which draws the clients into the experience. This is a central theme of this book, as of the Pine and Gilmore offering.

Questions can be raised about the metaphor. Can experience be a product? Is a properly designed environment enough? What is required in terms of preparation, personal facilitation, social organization, and symbolic introduction? Consider the tourism dilemma. In general tourists seem to seek a new experience in a familiar and protected presentation. Novelty and safety may be difficult to combine in a tour or destination, especially when much of the environment is out of control. Travelers seek the challenge of new experiences with a minimum of risk. The extent to which a leisure experience can be designed and predetermined is tested in big business developments such as Las Vegas.

However, one element of the theater metaphor is beyond question. As in the theater, the leisure business environment is designed and operated to maximize positive and involving experiences. And one advantage that big business enjoys is that, again with Disney World as the epitome, they can control all or most of the environment and change what is not working.

Question: *In the business you are considering, are significant elements of the total process out of your control? If so, how can you mitigate possible negative results?*

Hint: Are there elements more in the control of the client? If so, how can you facilitate this?

Follow-up: How much of the experience should be left open?

Disney Was Right!

Not about everything, but about the target market for a leisure business. The target market is generally the small group—not only the family as Walt envisioned but also the variety of groups suggested in the previous chapter. It is a "small world" after all. Not in culture as the song suggests, but in where people really live most of their lives. The attention of most people most of the time is no more than a few people away. We may care about

We may care about a wider circle, but we tend to live in rather small social worlds.

a wider circle, but we tend to live in rather small social worlds.

The implications for a LB involve not only marketing but also management and design. If people want to be alone, they generally don't need a leisure business. There is the walk, the park, the library, and the theater as well as the residence. The leisure business is most often oriented to a small group, either brought to the site or created on-site in the activity process.

In those small worlds, no two lives are alike. "Stuff" happens. There is divorce, illness, death, children and spouses with special health needs, accidents, layoffs, business-required moves, and all the contingencies that disrupt life. All the schemes for identifying and categorizing people into market segments ignore these realities of life. In their immediate worlds of relationships and involvements, no two individuals have the same small worlds. Further, those worlds are always changing, sometimes slowly and sometimes in unpredictable events.

It is not heartless to think of how leisure investments, associations, timetables, skills, and anything that help people rebuild may become crucial to clients. Rather, when work, family, or other associations central to the small worlds are disrupted, leisure may become central to the process of healing. It may not be realistic to see those in such forced transitions as a "target market," but being sensitive to the presence and needs of such people is not only good business practice; it is making a leisure business more than a place to play.

Especially for older clients, one aspect of this awareness is the potential therapeutic value of a leisure activity for those who have had a health trauma and are on the road back to full functioning. Sometimes friends and family provide needed support in the recovery process, but often they are unable to function in a skill-based environment. Sports devotees often do not want to abandon their sport after a heart attack but need help in getting back into it slowly. It may not qualify as a market, but it can be a real LB function.

But for the Small Business, It May Be a Big World

On the other hand, many small businesses do not live in an isolated world protected from the big guys. There are many examples.

Big Box

The first for small businesses is the "big box." In sports, camping, apparel, and other leisure activity-related items, the big store down the road may sell your product ... and with "lowest prices always." In many cases, the manufacturers and distributors collaborate in this competition by making low-cost racquets, clubs, tents, and so on for the big boxers. When a Wilson, Prince, or Head tennis racquet is $24 at Walmart and one that looks the same is $175 at the pro shop, why would a beginner not go for price? Golf clubs, balls, bags, shoes, jackets, and so on are there, too. An experienced player may know the difference, but many do not. One answer is just to concede the low-end market to the big boxes, but that is a great loss of market share.

Small Box

Then, for most leisure items there are the online suppliers, the computer "small box." Tennis and golf pro shops, bookstores, and sports clothing retailers, for example, have just had to swallow their annoyance at seeing their regulars walk in with new equipment purchased from the national online suppliers. The onliners can offer a complete line of manufacturers, brands, and models. They can have discounts, sales, and clearances that no small local retailer can approach. What is really frustrating for the on-site business is when customers even browse and try out items and then buy them elsewhere. Right or wrong, it's just a fact of retailing in almost any business except those that offer on-site services. The world of retailing has now gone global online with the aid of the worldwide efficient delivery services and their incredible computerized logistics. For any sports equipment, leisure apparel, outdoor gear, instruction literature and visuals ... anything that can be showcased online and delivered in a truck ... the competition is from a Big World of business.

Capital

There are many kinds of leisure businesses that require very large outlays of capital. Destination resorts, manufacturing of machine-tooled equipment, national or global advertising and distribution, travel packages that involve river and ocean cruising ... anything large scale requires big-time capital. Financing becomes a matter of packaging loans, collateral, professional design and management, and so on up in the nine-figure stratospheres. The good news is that there are lots of jobs in such operations. The bad news is that most entry-level opportunities are, for the most part, low wage, insecure, often seasonal, and dead end. Some even require the worker to be relatively young and attractive.

... big businesses have their own problems.

Of course, some big businesses create opportunities for auxiliary businesses. The major resort may contract out various services or rent space for small businesses. The problem is that they usually hold on to the major profit centers. On the other hand, rented space reduces capital outlays and consequent risk. It can be an opportunity.

In the Big World, Is Big Business Where the Opportunities Are?

For some areas, the answer is clearly "Yes." Just capital requirements alone make this a fact. Securing major capital investment from banks, venture capital, and investment trusts calls for more than a good idea and enthusiasm. Some space and equipment can be leased. Some franchises come with capital sources. Some investments can be bought at 30 cents on the dollar following first-generation failure. (This works only when a viable business fails due to undercapitalization.) But the big ones are out there and not likely to go away.

On the other hand (this again), big businesses have their own problems. Probably the main one is overinvestment in the status quo. It can be nearly impossible for an established leadership team to be receptive to a "There may be a better way of doing this" approach. I can cite my own experience with corporations such as General Motors (in their set-in-stone management days) or Yamaha (when lack of flexibility cost them millions) as examples. For the most part, corporate leaders do not really want a new perspective. They tend to rehire consultants who tell them what they want to hear. They keep bright young thinkers on the periphery of real decisions. And, at the same time, they choke out competition. Exceptions? Sure, but don't wait around too long.

Is there a place in the leisure business spectrum for innovation? Absolutely. But don't expect it to be easy, even when you have facts and figures to support your argument. Kahneman (2011) cites being "risk averse" as only the beginning of becoming unable to see how things might be different ... and better. As a result, trying to implement some of the ideas from this book is likely to be dismissed if heard at all.

In such situations, the issue is what is called "corporate culture." If you stumble on a corporation in which innovation and self-criticism are the norm, call yourself blessed and apply for a job. However, you may not want to be self-supporting until you find one.

Question: *Can you think of successful innovations in the LB field?*

Clue: Cast a wide net ... oceans away and down the road.

What Do "Experts" Know?

In any field of business, there are those who sell their expertise. In some cases, they have a financial interest in what they are promoting. The obvious examples are the trade associations that exist by promoting their activity/product. In a recession with grounded forecasts negative, they usually project that next year will see the "beginning of a recovery" every year until eventually they are right.

Often more persuasive are those with the latest "great new idea." Of course, some of them are right; the idea really is great. Others have one foot in the air and the other on a very slippery soapbox. As previously suggested, the best way to critique the dreamers is with the baseline numbers and trends and with a bunch of hard questions. If the enthusiast eventually blows you off with something like "You just don't get it," you can just agree. Hard questions ought to be the entrepreneur's bread and butter.

What About New Products?

To begin with, it is not always easy to differentiate innovation from promotion. A few hints are in order at this point:

*   Baseline statistics and observation are two entries into what people really do. For the most part, most people don't change much.

*   Again, begin your analysis of possibilities with what is known about what people really do. There are exceptions, but most successful innovations in some way improve the experience of what people are doing now rather than require radical change of timetables, skills, associations, or satisfactions.

    Change comes hard for most people most of the time.

*   If some change would be required, look hard at assertions that people will change. WHY? What would be a powerful enough inducement to change? What would have to be given up? What would be the barriers to adoption of something new? Change comes hard for most people most of the time. There are exceptions, but why this one?

There is the complex and ongoing case of electronics and miniaturization. The technical innovations are great and continual. I can hold in my hand more power than would have filled a room at the beginning of my academic career. Nanotechnology, they tell us, will make everything electronic faster, smaller, more portable, and more powerful ... in months not years.

Along with this comes communication possibilities. Computing is one thing. Calculating is possible for anything binary ... or whatever. There is the excitement, accessibility, and immediacy of connecting electronically. There are also considerable risks. For those who love game playing, not everyone, the expansion of opportunity is exciting and wildly attractive. It is, in the terms we have been using, an engrossing, challenging, and flow-inducing experience. Of course, the development and expansion are literally exponential.

We are embodied, physical and material beings who do not live entirely in the mind.

But is it real? Many questions are yet to be answered about diversion from other kinds of learning, other more direct ways of connecting, and saturation in appeal that calls for ever-new devices and programs. Perhaps more significant are the limitations. We are embodied, physical and material beings who do not live entirely in the mind. The mind–body relationship seems unbreakable and essential. We are also social beings. What happens on the court or course, in the outdoors, in the rhythm and touching of dance, and in the bedroom cannot be reproduced electronically. All leisure experiences cannot be enabled with any device or program, even with tactual representations in 3-D. The fact that we are embodied suggests one approach to LB investment that is unlikely to disappear.

9

THE LITTLE PICTURE

Some of the hype about small business is a bit deceptive. It is unquestioned that over half fail in less than two years. Most failure estimates are higher. Touted as "job creators," about half of small businesses employ no one. They are staffed entirely by their owners and often family. This includes many leisure businesses that are local and provide on-site services. Many are also seasonal.

Even small businesses face complications. They report revenues and pay taxes. If they have employees, they become involved in reporting employee incomes and paying payroll taxes. They have concerns about health care and retirement. Decisions regarding structure such as the advantages of a limited liability partnership or corporation may be made based on tax codes that can change at any time. Insurance, when obtainable, can be expensive. And there are all the issues of seasonality, location, competition, financing, and accounting that require careful consideration.

. . . about half of small businesses employ no one.

Given all this, there remain possibilities for a LB that can be exciting, profitable, and possessing growth potential. In this chapter, some of the possibilities will be explored. This will not, however, be a catalog of the range of viable businesses but a set of perspectives from which to develop a strategy.

Target Markets Revisited

One type of target market can be national or global. If the business is based on a particular activity-facilitating product, then it may best be marketed on the Internet. Establishing a website, with or without the assistance of specialists (also located on the Internet search engine), is the beginning. The website should feature exactly how and why the product is different. Text and pics should be oriented to those who are in the 20–25% who do the activity regularly. In some cases, the product may enhance the experience for almost anyone who does the base activity. In more cases, it will improve the experience for those already adept and dedicated.

The big advantage of this business strategy is its low cost. Hooking up with something such as PayPal, targeted websites, and a reliable distribution service can keep initial costs confined to the development and production of the item (along with patenting if advisable). In some cases the market may be so specific that narrowly focused journals and outlets will reach a high proportion of the target. In others, more Web ingenuity is required.

... promotion is best designed by those who know the nature of that experience.

The focus of promotion should always be what the product does to enhance the play experience. Such promotion is best designed by those who know the nature of that experience. However, it is important to seek a range of those who do the activity rather than assume that one's own approach is universal.

At the other end of the market spectrum is the local business. It may be located in the center of a set of users who then take their purchases to a variety of locations. Or it may be at or near a prime site for doing the activity. In either case, as introduced previously, location is critical. A side street or failing strip mall may offer a tempting rental. However, what is saved in rent will often be more than offset by the costs of promotion. Even a good billboard can run more than rental savings.

Many successful leisure businesses are "piggybacks." That is, they provide a useful service near a prime activity site such as a beach, ski slope, rock face, public facility, school or college, or whatever draws participants. Again, a careful assessment of the size and accessibility of the target market is required. A unique or different service may create some new market possibilities, but those old baseline numbers are important for any strategy.

The core of a marketing strategy is the experience. The questions of what people do, how they do it, and how choices are made have to be asked and answered from as many sources of information and analysis as possible. Promotion and location follow trying to answer these often hard questions. The remainder of this chapter will offer some clues to answering these questions.

"Specialties": Small Markets and Surprising Profits

Back to those specialty activities that have a small number of regular participants, usually less than ½ of 1% of the adult population, but that still offer viable markets in the right time and place. Some specialties require a special environment that may draw amateurs (i.e., lovers of the activity) to that special location. Already mentioned are windsailing in the Columbia River gorge, soaring near hilly terrain with wind, climbing at rock faces, and certain backcountry activity.

One surprising enterprise was begun by a mountain biker in the snow belt. No doubt listening to the complaints of his fellow bikers, he developed a concept for an indoor mountain bike park in the Milwaukee area. A number of factors worked for him. One was a concentration of outdoor off-road bikers in the area. A second was the availability of large warehouse-type buildings empty due to the recession. Third was his technical knowledge that enabled him to design a complex and varied set of runs. Fourth was a strategy that took into account that this was a counter-season business so that income had to be gained in that season, four to six months depending on weather.

This strategy was based on the entrepreneur's intimate knowledge of the sport and what made it attractive. However, even in Wisconsin the market was limited to the core participants in a low-numbers activity. It was a niche market for a niche activity. An indication of the validity of the scheme is the distance some come to use the facility. Would it work elsewhere? Not in many locations. Is the sport at the peak of its activity life cycle? That would require some careful research to begin to answer, even though various forms of cycling are currently growing in participation.

There are, no doubt, other such niche possibilities.

There are, no doubt, other such niche possibilities. Some are local. Some require a very careful assessment of the actual numbers of dedicated clients with feasible access to the location. Initial analysis includes specialty dedicated markets, "flow" experience and the conditions that enable it, and possible organizations of related amateurs and their locations. Are there risks? Of course, but such niche markets may be among the most reliable when fads are recognized and avoided.

At the center of such markets is the devotion of clients to the activity. Many are the amateurs who define themselves within the activity. They often devote remarkable portions of their incomes to the activity, even placing housing and clothing in distant second places. There has long been a recognition of devotees who are "horse poor." Maybe there are those who are "Harley poor," "book or art poor," or even golf poor.

Big Markets in Small Places

Contrasting to niche markets for activities with small numbers are special opportunities for large number activities. It is the "If you build it, they will come" myth. However, the "field of dreams" can turn into the "sinkhole of nightmares." Again, beware of promoters such as those who have hawked sports arenas in midsize cities with promises of attracting growth and ancillary investment. Many arenas now sit largely empty, devouring tax dollars, not entirely victims of a recession.

Among other factors ignored were operating costs, difficulties of attracting home teams, and the constant competition of sports on television.

Nevertheless, there are big number niches. Many depend on special environments. For example, even with golf courses closing and country clubs bankrupt, a really stunning design in a gorgeous location operated at modest cost may attract those tired of urban crowds and membership pressures at the private club. Now national syndicates are buying formerly private clubs and using their marketing and operational strategies to attract wider, especially younger, clienteles. Of course, overbuilding in a boom and failure to recognize that peaks are followed by declines can lead to a lot of failures. If you build it, they may go somewhere else or just not do it.

The catch is, of course, competition.

The major draw for a business based on large-participation activities is the base numbers. A specialty activity may have only 100,000 players across the country. An activity such as golf may have a total over 20 million, bowling 25 million, running/jogging 32 million, and even tennis over 10 million (U.S. Census Bureau, 2012). Even applying the 80-20 rule on frequency, that's a lot of people. Numbers for gardening, reading, and walking are even higher. Then there are over 65 million boaters, 12 million hunters, 25 million freshwater fishers, and 60 million visits to ski slopes. That's a lot, even recognizing some declines during a recession and glutted markets for resale boats and other recreation items.

The catch is, of course, competition. As previously argued, competition is everywhere. For equipment and apparel, there are the big boxes and the small boxes (online). In many areas so many destination resorts have been developed that markets are saturated, and savvy investors are looking for the twice-bankrupt at fire sale prices. "One more" in many market areas may be one too many. Three successful businesses in an area may saturate the market so that the fourth will flop.

There are, however, opportunities for the clever and resourceful who really know the nature of the base activity:

- One is to analyze what the big businesses don't offer around the edges. Supplementary services may do quite well near the big resort, federal or state recreation areas including wilderness access points, or as a regional supplier of high-end items where quality is paramount in buying decisions.

- Another is high-quality instruction in an activity, again in a location where markets are of adequate size. You don't have to own a ski resort to gain a reputation as the best teaching pro around ... or a concert hall to teach piano or woodwinds, a boatyard to renovate older models, or a factory to specialize in Harleys or Sekais ... in the right location

- The best facility may not be the biggest. It may be impossible to compete with the big guys at the major locations, but what about small ski slopes near a city, a ceramics studio for those out of school, or a small fitness center near a large working population who can get out of the office or lab for an hour at odd hours?

There are online specialty outlets for walkers and joggers who require high quality and carefully designed shoes. Adapted chairs for "wheelie" sports. Travel organizers for clients with specialty interests, preferably with discretionary income to spend. The trick is to know the activity, the modes of participation, and the nature of related experiences. The big businesses are not always good at details.

One strategy is building on someone else's success somewhere else.

Competition means that if you build it, someone else may already be there. Expanding a business is usually cheaper than starting a new one. Plus an established leisure-based business already has a hold on a significant market share.

One strategy is building on someone else's success somewhere else. Identifying successful businesses and their strategies can be a big head start for a different location. Again, it is crucial to analyze the market base.

Another strategy is to build on someone else's failure. A good concept may be ruined by poor operation or by inadequate financing. Failure is a big warning, but there are times and places that a business can be purchased or leased at a discount and renewed by management that has identified problems that can be remedied.

Question: *Do you know of any second-chance LB successes?*

Clue: Look first at major market areas.

Dilemmas of Design and Operation

One balancing act for a leisure business is between the security of a "no surprises" approach versus the challenge of something new and different. From a flow perspective, a regular and even familiar context may be essential to achieving a high level of involvement. Wild winds can disrupt the skill–challenge pairing in an outdoor sport. In indoor settings, disruptive activity in the area can prevent full concentration. Management of a leisure environment requires attention to the regular conditions that enhance the experience.

On the other hand (again), too much familiarity can produce boredom.

On the other hand (again), too much familiarity can produce boredom. Just making the same ceramics bowl over and over, playing the same opponent for a year, or hiking the same trail 50 times can deteriorate what was formerly a good experience.

Uniqueness versus familiarity can be a dilemma in LB design and operation. How can an artificial climbing wall not become boring? How can a theme park not become too familiar? Of course, finding new challenge is largely up to the client. She can seek new opponents or companions, try different techniques, learn new skills, and take risks in the leisure process. For the business provider, it is important to control disruptive or overutilized environments while also enabling new experiences and challenges. Grading the difficulty of ski slopes and trails is a clue to such management.

Question: *Are there ways to achieve a balance between reliability and novelty in leisure settings?*

Hint: Strategies may involve other people as well as design.

The next chapter offers some perspectives on management that enhance the client's experience. For the most part, it is based on research into leisure experiences and satisfactions. However, it is probably worthwhile to remind ourselves that we need to watch and listen carefully when clients are coming, playing, and leaving for indications of having had a "great time." Watching can be unobtrusive. Occasionally a follow-up question after an expression of satisfaction can guide the manager to an improved operation. "Watch and listen" is not just for crossing the street.

Competition Around the Edges

When exploring the "small business" scene, there are often opportunities around the edges. That is, a major set of activities or provisions may involve a sizable market that is not being fully met. For example, a burgeoning youth soccer program may need servicing for equipment, repairs, instruction in the off-seasons, or even tournament transportation. Some markets seem more than adequately met by the big boxes, but don't be too sure. Gardening supplies and equipment inventories from the big guys tend to be regional or even national. The special requirements of a local area can often be missed.

When exploring the "small business" scene, there are often opportunities around the edges.

The point is simple: Activities that involve a lot of people are not necessarily supported in all aspects by established businesses, however sophisticated their computer systems.

How does one locate such "edge" opportunities? Probably by counting the base numbers and then observing and asking. Often such niche markets are known best by those already involved in the activity and locale. A warning, however, may be in order. Don't get carried away by your own enthusiasm to project an "everyone will want to do it" approach.

Who Isn't There: Research On Not Doing It

I'll have to be honest here. Not much research attention has been given to *not* engaging in any leisure activity. However, there has been some study of blocking and inhibiting factors. Some are self-evident and need no more than mention here. Others may be a bit more tricky.

The Big Inhibitors: Time and Money

Many people who would like to take up an activity or do it more just don't have the time. In one study in Oregon, we interviewed a single mom of three children running a restaurant whose 8 a.m. to midnight schedule just didn't include anything done for anticipated satisfaction in doing it. She may have been an extreme, but lack of predictable time for discretionary activity is the single most common inhibitor for leisure.

As suggested previously, there are ways of responding to this problem. The first is flexible operation schedules. The second is identifying time-starved

. . . more peak time is overlapping than separate.

persons who could be accommodated with some programmatic adjustments and innovations. The third is to design and locate for time-efficiency. While some clients want a place to hang out, others want to have a quick in and out. Both markets are important.

The money issue is somewhat different. A very large proportion of the population simply can't afford much if any leisure with significant cost. In her study of laid-off steelworkers, Lisa Raymond found that one of the first things they gave up was going to ball games, despite the free time forced on them.

However, there are ways of meeting even this blocker. Some low-income clients have time flexibility and can become secondary markets for off-peak hours at reduced cost. Unfortunately, as more economic sectors have schedules similar to schools and other retailers, more peak time is overlapping than separate. Everyone, including students, wants the 5 to 10 playing times in the late afternoons and evenings. Flex schedules among some retailers and services can open times for some that can be offered at cut prices.

What is evident is that time and money frequently combine to be a double barrier to leisure engagement.

Social Factors

Many activities are done with groups rather than alone. Generally, these groups are not made up of strangers. A leisure business can frequently enlarge markets in two ways: One is to facilitate participation by "natural groups" such as families and work associates. A second is to provide ways, often no more complex than a coffee and conversation area, in which clients can meet and develop relationships. (If this seems to contradict the "time scarcity" problem, it is only a reminder that markets for the same activity in the same place may be quite varied.) And on-site child care is not outmoded, regardless of changing household configurations.

> **... a leisure setting brings together people with at least one, and often several, things in common.**

Leisure and the "New" Urban Associations

A counter-market is found mostly in urban areas where there are lots of strangers, persons not tied into social networks. Many different kinds of activity can be venues for meeting others. An important factor is that a leisure setting brings together people with at least one, and often several, things in common. Churches used to provide such a social setting, and still do for some. Now, however, in this time of "unmarriedness" leisure serves the same purpose for many. For the LB manager, providing times and places for interacting may be more important for attracting and retaining clients than the efficiency of getting people in and out fast. There is a whole new industry of helping people meet that may be much more successful in places of mutual activity than on the World Wide Web.

Learning Skills and Gaining Satisfactions

Note the overlap here with the previous concept. Generally, as skills increase in any activity, so do satisfactions. Near the top of most lists of "why I don't do ..." is a lack of skill. Most business providers of leisure activity have learning programs central to their overall offering. What may be difficult is to provide "upgrades" as well as introductions. One has to know the skills of an activity very well to calibrate upgrades and offer them in ways attractive to their clients. However, they have a secondary benefit in increasing participation. They build personal satisfactions in skill development and potential flow, and they also bring together activity associates of similar levels of advancement.

In the next chapter, the focus will be on client-focused management with some of the issues and possibilities of this chapter as background.

10

SERVICING THE EXPERIENCE

Is experience a commodity, something that can be designed, labeled, packaged, and sold in the same way for all consumers? Or is it changing, shifting, and even individualized? The answer is clearly the latter. "Delivery" of the possibility of leisure experience is a process, not a product. Therefore, leisure business is a kind of service industry with client-oriented management that is constantly sensitive to what is occurring ... and not occurring.

The theater metaphor previously mentioned (Pine & Gilmore, 1999) is useful in its focus on performance and the reception of the client. It suggests that in a leisure context there are many roles to be played. The focus, however, is on the receivers who also are active in the process. The leisure experience is never just receptive, passive. It is an involving process in which the players are all acting in one way or another. The business managers are not just presenting but are also making possible the roles of active participation. In the end, the aim is peak experiences for the clients.

One implication is that the provider roles may vary. Some engage closely with the players in enhancing the experience. Others provide an environment and stay out of the way. In any case, the aim is to maximize the involvement and satisfaction of the clients. What follows is an analysis from a wide range of research on elements of satisfying leisure experiences and ways of enhancing them.

Components of Leisure Experience

One question concerns how we can gain an understanding of the components of good leisure experiences. Is there a way of summing up a process that may go on for hours or even days? Almost all questionnaire research assumes that at the end of an event or even days later in response to a written or online set of questions, the leisure participant can sum up the quality of the event or environment. The obvious problem is that any experience of duration will rise and fall in satisfaction, even from minute to minute. Summations are not usually a good way to sort out and identify the components that produce highs and lows. Questionnaires have value, but they are too abstracted to tap immediate elements. Furthermore, there is a lot of research on how the order, wording, and context of summation questions can radically influence responses. Nonetheless, since it is recollections that provoke return business, they can be useful.

... any experience of duration will rise and fall in satisfaction ...

A second approach is called "experience sampling." As introduced earlier, it involves using a device to interrupt whatever is going on at random times to answer questions about "right now." Of course, one immediate problem is that the experience is already interrupted rather than ongoing. However, it avoids many of the problems of the summation of "On the whole, how would you rate your trip to the ... ?"

Experience sampling has often focused on the question of when people are happiest. The management clues that follow are based to a large extent on the findings of such an approach. Already suggested are the findings that people tend to be most satisfied when they are active rather than passive, when they are in the flow of skill and challenge, and when they are with people with whom they have positive ongoing relationships. These findings are consistent across almost any kind of leisure environment and activity. However, probably no two kinds of activity or settings facilitate these satisfactions in just the same way ... not to mention for different people.

Managing for Experience

Can flow be manufactured? Can we organize an event so people enjoy each other? Are meanings and emotions programmable? The answer is, of course, "Not really." No program can guarantee any particular result when there are real people involved, especially people in groups. Any individual comes to an occasion with a complex set of histories, evoked emotions, and idiosyncrasies. Group interaction is a process in which combinations of actions and reactions create ever-new environments. The quality of the experience is "emergent," not predetermined.

Can flow be manufactured?

However, there are research-based clues about how to enhance experiences and maximize positive outcomes. Such clues also can help the manager avoid negative outcomes. These clues concern designed environments, approaches to enabling an experience, and a few programmatic approaches. Leisure, by definition, is to a great extent open ended. We may refer to leisure business "providers," but more accurately they are "enablers." Nevertheless, there are designs, styles, communication modes, and responses that can make a difference. Some no doubt will be found in entrepreneurial texts, often with somewhat different vocabularies. In this case, we will begin with the social and behavioral studies.

First, the "End Effect"

Kahneman (2011) reports research that has found that "end effects" have disproportionate weight in evaluating an experience. The entire leisure event contributes to evaluation, and high and low points may occur at any point. However, the ending is especially significant. The leisure manager cannot control events so that every participant wins the last point, receives the final applause, or has the final product rise above the quality norm. If it could be externally manipulated, it would thwart the uncertainties that are central to many leisure experiences. However, there are some elements that would apply to almost any business management.

Tour operators do not offer a closing dinner just out of generosity. That final event is intended to allow travelers to reinforce each other in recalling the high points of a trip. The risk is that discomforts and conflicts may be recalled as well. The strategy of designing a program toward a "high" ending is almost always a good one.

In an indoor provision, attention can be given to the leaving experience. Personal recognition and return affirmations are always good. Managers should instill on their front desk personnel the importance of arrivals and departures met with smiles, name recognition, and, when possible, a personal element.

Probably less commonly recognized are the design aspects of the end-stage experience. How many leisure providers skimp on things such as chat areas and even shower and changing spaces? Can a great game have a reduced impact in a dingy shower or a smelly locker room? Of course, since cold showers can lead to frozen faces and cold memories.

This does have to mean extra expense or making it all "fancy." The author conducted a user survey at an indoor tennis facility some years ago when the operator was thinking about upgrading the space at considerable cost. The overwhelming results of the survey were that the players wanted the most tennis at the lowest viable cost. Their priority for improvement was better lighting in the play area to enhance the central experience. Nevertheless, attention to departures can yield high returns on the dollar.

Related to this is knowing when not to sell. A positive experience can be alloyed by a persistent effort to sell at the departure. You want clients to remember how good they felt on the way home, not an annoyance or intrusion. In this economic culture where efforts to promote and sell are continual, discretion and judgment as to when NOT to may be just as important as developing an attractive promotion program.

Question: *What are the most important departure elements in your LB concept?*

Clue: Distinguish the personal from the environmental.

Leisure Is Personal

At the beginning, a design that symbolizes welcome can often be obtained with minimal expense. Spaces that are welcoming are open, light, and have meeting areas. Personal greetings are important for anyone and especially for those who are new or hesitant.

Almost all leisure businesses are dealing with people in groups of varying size and composition. In some cases, all who come together will play together. More often, activity groups meet at the site so that meeting spaces are crucial. They should

. . . meeting spaces are crucial.

be open and accessible, not hard to locate, and with décor and furnishings that signal welcome and social inclusion. The details will vary with the activity, social groupings, and space that is adaptable. But the aim of facilitating "gathering" is central.

The Dropout Problem

Research suggests at least two partial responses to the constant problem of clients who begin a program and then disappear. One is social and the second is endemic to the play experience. The dropout rates in many programs exceed 80% in relatively short periods of time. Exercise and fitness centers commonly have dropout rates so high that some develop pricing programs to get as much money as possible up front with the likelihood that they may not have to provide for most new clients in a few weeks or months. Assuming that the long-term success of a business is better served by retaining clients, what can be done to improve retention rates?

The first strategy is social. Leisure participants are most likely to stay in programs and not to miss regular times when they are part of a group. There are double factors: the positive enjoyment of the group and meeting their expectations. Anything a manager can do to encourage and facilitate the formation of play groups with a regular schedule will reduce both dropouts and absentees. Of course in competitive sports where numbers are essential the social factor is especially salient. Making it convenient to reserve regular times and even giving group discounts may pay off for the business.

. . . what can be done to improve retention rates?

The second strategy is based on the research of Ed McAuley of the University of Illinois. He has repeated studies demonstrating that experiencing "efficacy" is central to continuing an activity. This means simply that people tend to stay with an activity in which they feel they do well and/or are improving their skills. Goals should be challenging but reachable. This ties into the flow approach for skill-based activities. For others, the goals may be other outcomes such as health and fitness or some social recognition.

In both cases, management involves more than just providing an opportunity and stepping aside. Effective management involves "being there" and recognizing how experiences can be enhanced and consolidated.

Who Is Acting?

It is not cynical to recognize that in a sense everyone is putting on a show. That is, everyone is presenting a kind of self in ways that will create desirable responses from others. We not only think about appearance but also even more choose how we speak, respond, and interact with some sense of how others will see us and respond. Implications for the front-line personnel of a LB are obvious. However, it is also part of the leisure experience for clients.

The idea is not that a leisure site should be managed so that people can show off ... at least not too much. However, opportunities for some display can add to the positive experience. In an arts program, rotating displays and programs of affirmation can be graded in ways that give recognition to improvement. In sports it is a bit trickier. "Leader boards" and rankings have bottoms as well as tops that may discourage

... in a sense everyone is putting on a show.

engagement. A careful attention to improvement at any level of skill and interaction that calls attention to intrinsic satisfaction can enhance the experience for beginners and the less adept.

The sometimes hidden point is that people are constantly looking at the responses of others and finding satisfaction when they seem positive. Any activity participant knows to take opportunities to applaud and encourage others, especially those in the lower end of the learning curve. For the serving personnel of a business, opportunities for such responses should consistently be sought and created.

Is Everyone a Winner?

Of course, all this can go too far. For a learner to be overpraised or unrealistically evaluated renders the attempt meaningless. However, it is a primary task of LB service personnel to look for legitimate opportunities for approval as well as to design the program so that there can be successes at any level. And the more spontaneous the approval, the more authentic it seems.

The words and phrases, along with body language and tonal inflection, should be drilled into front-line leisure service providers at any level:

"Great ... job, shot, or anything else!"

"Looking good out there today!"

"Everyone enjoys playing ... with you!"

"Remember the good days (results, product) when things don't go quite so well."

"Always good to see you come through that door!"

Affirmation can come in so many forms. Sometimes a good smile says more than words. "Wow" might say more than an analysis of a good production or result. All this isn't being phony; it is just being the kind of leisure companion that often makes or breaks an experience. Remember that it is the experience you are selling, not just the activity itself.

Question: *Come up with an affirming approach that would work for your business.*

Hint: Different strokes for different folks.

Affirmation can come in so many forms.

Clue: Everyone isn't a winner … or can they be?

Beyond Hedonism

One of my colleagues complained years ago at the failure of those who study leisure and recreation to employ the term "fun." It was a point well taken. Complex analysis of motivations and satisfactions may obscure that many choices are just an anticipation of having fun. Kahneman (2011) is right that System 2 analysis of interrelated meaning dimensions is unlikely in most leisure decisions.

However, having fun may be more than an emotion. Rather, the emotion seems to be a consequence of some elements of an experience. A continual question for a leisure manager should be "What did I do or could I do to support my clients having fun?" Then we are immediately into trying to understand just what that experience can be and how a business design and operation can enhance those positive factors. Satisfaction doesn't just happen, even in play. Rather it is a process with components that rise and fall in significance. Summation evaluations often fail to identify the more immediate elements. In fact, even experience sampling that takes random slices of a total process is as likely to miss both the peaks and the

… having fun may be more than an emotion.

valleys as not. That is why a manager needs to be sensitive to any and every clue that could point to a managerial improvement.

Opportunity Outside the Box

I will not belabor the importance of critical observation again except to put it at the front of the line of information-gathering techniques. There are also some clues that may help you understand what is really going on out there.

First, in observation there is the problem of a false focus. If we focus only on the "official" activity, such as learning, competing, or producing something, we may miss the "side bets" that are of major importance in the total experience. We have already suggested what many of them may be. Most are usually social and involve interaction in and around the central activity. Others may be more specific to the nature of an activity. Experimenting, exploring, and otherwise trying out new ways of engagement are significant to many. Environments that encourage trying things out by minimizing the costs of failure can lead to new peaks. Just getting away into a different environment can be very important, especially for those who feel homebound or office-bound. Just playing the game is not all that is going on.

> . . . there is the question of what people are NOT doing and would like to do.

Second, there is the question of what people are NOT doing and would like to do. Observation is probably of less help here. Sometimes we can see clients try out unconventional ways of engagement that suggest boredom. However, relaxed post-experience conversations that introduce a question that many never consider can also be useful. "I wonder if there is another way to do this?" may encourage participants to share that offbeat idea that they have been harboring and are reluctant to share. Some ideas are impossible or unlikely to produce a better experience. But all are worth listening to.

Third, beware of survey results claiming interest. In neighborhood questionnaires large numbers of respondents will tell you they would like a new swimming pool, running track, bicycle trail, or whatever. However, when built, few will change their habits and investments to become regular clients. Of course there is the matter of price. At some unrealistically low price, lots of people will do almost anything. But this is of little use to an entrepreneur. All sorts of things look potentially attractive when we don't have to consider what we would have to change, give up, or rearrange to do it. This does not mean that surveys are useless, but they always have to be put in the context of those baseline numbers of what people are doing now.

Fourth, just look around ... even far away. There are clues out there in what people are doing and how they do it that may lead to good business concepts. When older people bike in inconvenient and even risky places, they may be indicating a latent demand. When people travel to do something, they may be suggesting a market for something similar nearby. When older people no longer do something they had enjoyed earlier, they may have been forced out by circumstances or even ageist prejudices and be a market for renewal. Of course, asking about what might increase participation or get them back into something discontinued is always a possibility. Look and listen ... and try to lay prejudices aside.

Question: *Considering the demographics of your market area, what might be a new opportunity for a target market?*

Clue: Check for population shifts first such as age, household composition, or education level.

Associative Memory and Marketing

Leisure business marketing is usually quite specific to the activity base, population characteristics, and location. The old tourism 3 Ss of "sun, sand, and sex" don't even do it for tourism any more. However, there are some clues in the social psychology of decision making that can be useful.

Kahneman (2011) analyzes "associative memory" in decisions, especially the less analytical System 1 kind. What do we remember from a really satisfying experience? As already suggested, usually the highs and lows, the endings, and the companions. Those key recollections vary according to the experience: the social and physical environment, the nature of the activity, and our own level of involvement. In marketing strategies, clearly the aim is to call up the positive elements and repress the negative.

How do we remember? The process of associative memory is one in which signs and symbols are "tags" for elements of a total experience. Generally, when we recall a leisure, or any other, occasion, it is in relatively simple images, words and phrases, and delineated segments of the total. We do not go through a complex experience sorting out the positive from the negative in a hierarchical schema.

. . . there are some clues in the social psychology of decision making that can be useful.

When trying to attract clients, new or repeat, the aim is to identify and employ those symbols and vocabularies that tap the highs of satisfaction and do not inadvertently trigger negatives. In print and Web advertising, pictures are employed that not only attract attention but also direct consciousness to positive associations. The ability to do this requires knowing the nature of the experience thoroughly. It is unlikely that an ad expert who is only a consumer rather than someone involved will be able to do this. However, the requirements are much the same as for good management.

The trick is to identify those words and images that call forth the positive associations, especially the "highs." For tourism, they may well be what is called to mind by the properly populated beach. Attractive people are usually a good sign. However, they should not be extraordinary to the extent that they scare off clients. (Too many bikini models may not attract the mother who is making the destination choices.) The more the associations are specific to a business offering, the better. However, some businesses are providing access or enhancement of an experience with another environment whose depiction calls up the desired associations.

Again, the focus is on the experience and its special positive associations. And the center of both management and marketing is QUALITY.

11

BEATING THE ODDS

The theme of this penultimate chapter is simple: QUALITY, QUALITY, QUALITY!
If you know just what quality means for your LB strategy, then you can skip to the final chapter. But there may be a few approaches you haven't thought of yet.

Beyond Satisfaction: Something Special

Many resorts have come up with a "value added" concept that has set them apart from the competition. There is one with a Friday pig roast including family entertainment. There are those with field trips to nearby historic or archeological sites. There are some with special themes related to a sport or type of entertainment. I developed a concept for a "family resort" that would include protected children's activity programs that free parents for their golf or tennis, on-site play areas, pet friendly rooms, well-maintained beach areas, and suites designed for multigenerations.

Other types of leisure businesses can develop their own signature themes that not only are central to marketing but also set them apart from other similar businesses. Experienced tourism operators can seize on some aspect of their plans, often related to the destination environment rather than the travel itself. Local businesses, as already suggested, may analyze their target markets and develop a presentation that is specific in its appeal.

Most approaches are based on a business's thorough knowledge of its client base combined with understanding the site and activity combination they offer. The aim is to develop something special. It is just the opposite of buying into a franchise that directs an operation into well-proven provisions and styles that are essentially the same from one place to another. In fact, franchises require the local owner to do it their way and write their contracts to enforce their standards. The advantage is that clients know what to expect. The disadvantage is that the local business loses flexibility and the freedom to respond to local conditions and opportunities.

The aim is to develop something special.

How does the developer identify the "something special" that will not only distinguish one business from others but also maximize its draw and retention? Again, largely by observing … one's own business in action and also by visiting parallel businesses. Look for the sights and sounds of joy. Watch and listen. (Even put down this book and get out there where people are playing.)

The key concept is quality. Remember that no one has to do it. If the experience made possible by your business doesn't yield a high level of satisfaction, or fun, then in time it will fail. Looking good may get people in the door, but it will not bring them back.

Barriers to Satisfaction

Remember that almost all leisure businesses require clients to come back over and over. Furthermore, the best advertising is person to person. "How did you decide to come to our whatever?" "I heard about it from a friend."

What are barriers to satisfaction, to clients wanting to do it over and over?

- Not connecting with enjoyable associates, partners, opponents, and so forth.

- Being unable to gain or exercise needed skills.

- Becoming bored as the challenge level does not increase with skills.

- Finding the environment unattractive.

- Being unable to coordinate convenient schedules with availability.

- Increases in costs that provoke cost-benefits analyses.

- The attraction of a competing experience when the quality of the current one fades.

Many, perhaps most, leisure experiences are a process. They are not static in skills, challenges, companions, or development. The same client who expresses a high level of satisfaction early in the process may be ready to move on, and away from your business, when there are no opportunities for a more complex or challenging experience. One of the appeals of the computerized games array is that there is always something new to try and experience ... and usually at a reasonable price. Furthermore, the technologies offer something better with each iteration. Those games have come a long way from the simple weapons-aiming chips of the early developments.

The quality that attracted clients may not retain the same people. Furthermore, if there is disappointment, if a promise is not fulfilled, then those who don't have to do it will disappear. And, of course, that is everyone. And they will talk down your business in ways that no clever promotion can overcome for long.

The Fatal Bias

Kahneman (2011) has several ways of describing the fatal bias. One is the "halo" effect that says that "If it's mine, it's got to be good." Just facts are no deterrent to those who are in love with anything from a new relationship to a business plan. It is difficult to stand back when you are in love, even with a plan that entails financial risk.

Kahneman (2011) also offers the problem of "priming." There are words, images, histories, or relationships that prime our attitudes and judgments. We are predisposed to have a positive reaction to a proposition that comes packaged in positive recollections, images, symbols, slogans, or presenters. It may be sexist and ageist to select attractive young women to peddle drugs to male doctors, but they do prime favorably. The problem in business strategies is that it may work against us. Associating a strategy with our personal histories, possibly even not remembered consciously, can bias evaluation and lead to a failure of critical System 2 thinking.

The trick is to recognize your own biases.

The trick is to recognize your own biases. However, if it were that easy, we would all avoid the error and produce one success after another. However, recalling the business failure rates alone ought to place us on guard against our favorable biases. One way of dealing with the fatal priming bias will be offered at the end of this chapter.

Mapping the Market

Any kind of critical analysis based on fact is good. Some kinds of facts are relatively easy to obtain; others can be costly.

Anyone developing a business strategy who does not get out there and examine both successes and failures is doomed to add to those failure statistics. In the process, it is crucial to distinguish experts from promoters. Of course, if your informant has something to sell, all colors of flags are waving. On the other hand, real enthusiasm is a positive clue.

One basic question is "How do you get a realistic assessment of the market?" Step one is to measure the market by using geographically relevant census data as to household composition in your likely market area.

Second, the Statistical Abstract of the United States online will offer some form of trend data on many leisure activities. A basic problem, however, is that the totals are aggregate and tell almost nothing about frequency and duration. Remember the 80-20 rule for a realistic guide to those big numbers.

Third, if you have a lot of money, there are major marketing organizations that can do all sorts of analysis from quite good databases. The problem is that we are talking many thousands of dollars for even targeted analyses. The recreation trends analysis of several years ago (Kelly & Warnick, 1999) was based on an excellent yearly household survey that allowed for identification of a wide range of significant market-identifying indices. At that time, the data were made available to universities at minimal cost. That is no longer the case. However, if you are a major player with lots of financing, you can get such analysis from Experian Simmons or a similar market research organization. For example, SRI International has done major studies for hotel chains, airlines, and others with the money to spend. But the results are totally proprietary. (A colleague could not even show me the index.)

However, nothing substitutes for OPE—other people's experience.

Good trend analysis is valuable from two perspectives. It gives a clue as to activities that have peaked and are on the downward curve of the Activity Life Cycle. This is so important when the mass media tout some "latest craze" with no contextual analysis. On the positive side, trend analysis from reliable data can help identify activities that have settled at a stable plateau or have solid growth base.

However, nothing substitutes for OPE—other people's experience. Getting out there with your own critical observation and fearless questions can open and close whole new worlds of opportunity for a LB.

Who Wins? Risk Aversion or Optimistic Bias

It depends ... on what? Recall that the underlying aim is beating the odds of failure. It is difficult and possibly counter-productive to begin with an attitude of probable failure. However, the odds are what they are. How can the investor balance risk assessment and optimism?

Kahneman (2011) and others have found that for the most part, people tend to be "risk aversive." A variety of decision experiments have demonstrated that many, maybe most, decisions involving money are not a rational assessment of risk versus gain. Avoiding loss is valued more than greater gain even when the ratio is clearly in favor of the potential gain. Explanations vary, but the finding is very consistent.

However, there are thousands of entrepreneurs taking risks with their savings, time, reputations, and egos to begin or purchase businesses. Somehow a combination of factors overcomes risk aversion. Certainly a belief in the business concept and plan is fundamental. A reasonable hope for profit usually involves running sets of numbers. Added factors may be the satisfaction of being involved in a set of activities and having clients that one enjoys, living in a desirable environment, and having a measure of autonomy. Nonetheless, courage and optimism that can overcome risk aversion needs to be supported by careful System 2 analysis.

... there is also an optimistic bias.

Remember that there is also an optimistic bias. The halo of "It's my idea," the association with positive experiences, and the excitement of doing something new and self-expressive are all factors in taking risks. Such positive factors are necessary to evoke the necessary optimism and persistence. So, on balance, who wins? Personality aside, are there ways that System 2 can help the entrepreneur assess both risk and possibility?

Question: *What are the most determinative factors in the potential success (or failure) in your business strategy?*

Clue: Are there keys to quality ... or barriers to peak experiences?

Are There Sources of Help?

I hope that those who are this far into the discussion have a number of clues. Some are focused on the concept and on the likelihood of offering experiences of quality with all the elements previously introduced. Again, there is no substitute for QUALITY in every aspect of the business. No quality, no experience. No experience, no market. No one has to do it, remember?

Are there sources of help in decision making? (Most are repetition)

1. Examine businesses in noncompetitive locations and query their managers.

2. Read this and other books for questions as well as answers.

3. Get help in running numbers of capital requirements, operating expenses, accounting and other services, insurance, taxes, and other fixed costs.

4. Be realistic in estimating how long it will take to build a solid clientele.

5. Assess all the limitations of seasonality, competition near and far, markets and access, pricing limitations in relation to markets, and, always, the baseline numbers.

6. Be realistic with those who represent sources of OPM (other people's money).

When it comes to specifics, all we can do in a book is raise the questions and suggest where some answers may be found. Every entrepreneur has to develop the answers for a specific time and place. One warning: the shocking finding in case studies of leisure-based businesses, especially small ones, is that very few investors have done this. Especially when self-financed, plans that address the critical questions were found to be the exceptions.

Surprise! Against Our Subtitle

Yes, now I will recommend even going back to business school. This book is not about the nuts and bolts of business formation and operation. Business plans, financing, accounting, legal issues, taxation strategies, personnel assessment, income projections, and a host of other issues are the province of a good B school or substitute. You may not need an MBA to run a business, but there is a lot of basic knowledge the investor had better obtain one way or another. Of course, experience working in a similar business for a period will help. However, much of the financial infrastructure of a business is hidden even from employees.

Good entrepreneurship guides and courses can be invaluable. It is not the job of the bank or start-up venture capital organization to do your business plan for you. Bookkeepers and accountants do not give away their knowledge and experience. Even experienced employees tend to look out for themselves rather than the entire business. You have to learn somewhere, and schools are in the business of teaching.

However, *nothing takes the place of quality, and the experience is all you have to sell.*

Now, One More Strategy

Kahneman (2011) introduces a process that he says some say is worth the price of his (or my) book and more. In two pages (pp. 264–265) he introduces the *premortem.*

The technique is simple and may be utilized at any stage of business development. It is a kind of System 2 thinking that focuses on the most important issues in developing business strategies. The premortem involves gathering a small group of analysts, preferably more-than-average bright and with some relevant experience. Their task is to develop a scenario of failure.

Gather a group of knowledgeable people, preferably diverse in gender, age, and culture. Introduce your business concept and plan including expected markets, management style, and operations focus. Then ask the big question. "Assume that in a year (or two) the business has failed. Write a scenario (story) of how the failure occurred." Time should be limited, perhaps 10 to 20 minutes. Then read them aloud and discuss the implications for the plan, including possible remedies for potentially fatal problems.

Does this sound rather negative? Consider how negative you will feel if you develop a business that fulfills the stories. Finally, then, let's look ahead at some stability and change in which a new business will succeed or fail.

12

LOOKING AHEAD

First, there is the question about forecasting: Is it possible? Kahneman (2011) reports a series of studies on the reliability of predictions of experts and "pundits." The overall results are essentially zero. So, anything that follows should be read with a degree of fundamental skepticism. However, there is also the sociological adage that past behavior is the best predictor of future behavior. If you review the previous 11 chapters, you will find that almost all the analysis has been based on

The overall results are essentially zero.

actual behaviors, not speculation of self-appointed "futurists" or otherworldly philosophers. At least, this chapter on looking ahead will be largely based on facts.

The Optimistic Bias and "Black Swans"

As I write, there is a massive cruise liner still lying on its side just off the shore of an Italian resort island. Seemingly, the captain steered a course too close to reefs to showboat to those on the island. There were deaths, the loss of a great multi-decked cruise liner, and all sorts of fallout. The impacts on the Mediterranean cruise business are still to be calculated. Little facts that have come to light such as a design that is so top-heavy that recovery from a few degrees of list may be impossible, lifeboats that can't be launched from over 15 degrees of tilt, and a crew not trained for disaster management will not do the industry much good. Such an unexpected event is called a "Black Swan." It is a catastrophic happening that no one anticipates or prepares for. (It is also the case that when someone warns about such possible events, he is dismissed as ignorant or biased.)

However, there are such events that can impact the entire structure of an industry. In this case, how many potential cruise clients will picture that great ship lying there as they consider their next trip? Such unexpected associations are always a possibility. Some are enormous such as the impact of Katrina on the Gulf Coast tourism industry. Some are personal such as a bad experience with a rip tide making a beach vacation less attractive.

Another current example: With the "gaming" industry, did the promoters deliberately ignore the numbers or were they just as naïve as the politicians seeking revenue? After all, a casino with its built-in and guaranteed "hold" or house percentage has to be the most reliable profit center in the wide world of leisure businesses. The "nattering nabobs of negativity" who predicted an oncoming saturation of the markets as hundreds of new casinos were opened and proposed clearly were prejudiced. Just ask the developers of "Foxwoods" in Connecticut who expanded to the world's largest casino complex. Oops! Foxwoods is teetering on the edge of bankruptcy and can't figure out how to qualify for Chapter 11. Guess what? Even so, neighboring Massachusetts is considering legislation to tap their share of the Foxwoods "profits."

Considerable research has demonstrated that the economic benefits of gambling for the host area depend on attracting clients from outside the economic catchment zone. If nearly all gamblers at a casino, however fancy, are local then the money lost to other local businesses, including LBs, usually exceeds the tax gain from gambling revenue. This does not take into account social costs of addiction, divorce, crime, and other outcomes requiring remediation and protection services. The state of

Montana has minimized public gain from outside revenue and maximized local costs by licensing small local casinos rather than strategically located ones that attract outside money (i.e., losers).

Don't Upset Me With Facts

There is that nasty old WYSIATI ("What you see is all there is") again. When we are sure what will work, that tends to be all we see. Little facts such as the number of people within driving distance of a leisure site, the census estimate that 45% of them are poor or near poor, and the general declining trend of participation in

> **When we are sure what will work, that tends to be all we see.**

the base activity are, if known, overwhelmed by something we think we see.

Let me give the example of how I could have saved a nameless motorized sports machine company millions (Japanese name withheld to protect me from lawsuit), probably hundreds of millions, if they had taken my advice. They contracted for market advice on motorized winter sports machines. Examining the numbers for markets, I found growth in the rural market related to both work and pleasure. My recommendation was that they design safer products such as flexible four-wheelers that maximized safety and that had a dual use, on the farm and as a family activity that could tap an unrecognized market. This was not what the corporate decision makers wanted to hear. Committed to an image of speed and power, they went in the opposite direction. Then a rash of accidents and lawsuits came along that cost them millions in court costs, damages, and design changes. The point is not that I was so prescient, but that the company executives ignored numbers and stayed with their previous commitment.

Probably those reading this will not be in a position to make such a costly error based on WYSIATI and institutional inertia. However, at any level and on any scale, ignoring the numbers and a failure to take a critical look at accepted common wisdom can be costly. What follows is deliberately conservative. Go elsewhere for futurist dreamers who believe that anything that is technologically possible will happen. They have been proven wrong so often that their big book sales and speaking fees ought to be an embarrassment.

What Do We Know About the Future?

Absolutely, there will be both continuity and change. Most of the change will have central strains of continuity. Most of the continuity will contain elements of change. No trends will be "straight line." Social, economic, and political trends are zigzag, not linear. Even the most confident population forecasts of 20 years ago have proven about half right.

Social, economic, and political trends are zigzag, not linear.

Given that and focusing on leisure business issues, what are some of the most likely and relevant forecasts? (For a somewhat fuller analysis, see Chapter 12 in my *Leisure*, 4th edition.) The focus here will be on leisure business implications.

Economic Factors

Globalization. The travel industry no longer begins at the local agency, but is worldwide and online. Financing is worldwide for once-local developments. Communications and information are online and available to everyone everywhere.

Employment. Some structural unemployment will outlast recessions as automation replaces manufacturing workers and as labor-intensive production chases low wages. Human services and retailing will employ more women with a majority of mothers in the paid workforce. Skilled R&D (research and development) workers will be rewarded for their long hours and high pressure. For most, predictable "careers" will be supplanted by a series of jobs. Work schedules will be variable with more services operating 24/7.

Income and wealth. Those with wealth that produces income will continue to do well. Along with costly to replace skilled professionals, they will continue to receive disproportionate portions of income leaving the middle mass as well as the poor and near-poor further behind. As a result, high-end markets will receive the most leisure investment attention.

Value changes. For the affluent, the time–income tradeoff may shift somewhat in favor of leisure. However, the market focus on high-end leisure provisions and experiences will continue to have impacts. Will most believe that higher prices produce better experiences? Don't bet against it.

Political Factors

Leisure is unlikely to become a central political issue, at least as long as there is a struggle between those who give primacy to reducing government services and deficits and those who are committed to government services for those with high needs and low resources. However, there are some possible changes in priorities:

- Renewed attention to urban decay and poverty.

- Continued reliance on the market sector for most leisure provisions.

- Tax policies that support particular leisure resources such as the arts and give tax deductions to second homes and big toys used for business will be questioned.

- Comprehensive long-range planning may address issues such as land use and conservation with resources for recreation included as one factor in the planning. There will continue to be conflicts between planners and some developers, but cooperation in some sites.

- A continued trend toward cost-recovery in the administration of public recreation resources and programs.

Demographic Factors

The graying of America ... and most of the world. By 2030 over 20% of the U.S. population will be over 65, and the greatest percentage increase will be those over 75.

Fertility and family size. Declines in fertility rates slowed after 1990 due to the increase in various ethnic groups. However, delayed marriage for women, rising education levels, labor force participation of women, and early marriage divorce rates have reduced the number of children desired. Now the baby boom wave is passing into retirement years.

> Now the baby boom wave is passing into retirement years.

Household composition. Increases in female-headed households and a reduction in those headed by married couples to about 50% along with declining marriage rates are changing the old patterns of those seeking "family leisure."

Diversity. With half or more growth due to immigration, many new citizens will be from Latin America and southern Asia. Ninety percent of the growth has been in the South and Southwest.

Education. Education levels will increase but with disparities based on income. Higher education will be a growth industry.

Boomers. The "baby boom" bulge will create LB markets for the retired and then gradually disappear.

Family Factors

- Smaller families, instability, singleness, shorter periods of parenting, and increased female employment are all significant for leisure. The assumption of the familial household as the primary context of leisure may be changing, with uncertain consequences.

- More leisure may be invested in "non-couples" including single parents.

- Leisure may become a more important context of finding and developing relationships.

  More leisure may be invested in "non-couples"

- The two-parent assumption for children's recreation programs will be challenged.

Value-Orientation Factors

- The diminishing centrality of organized religion seems to open formerly "sacred times" to leisure.   Furthermore, leisure often replaces the church as a place of social bonding. Regional differences, however, remain significant.

- The preservation and appreciation of natural environments are emerging as mainstream rather than fringe, even though conflicts continue.

- Will an "experience ethic" for leisure continue to replace the former extrinsic rationales of health and productivity? Maybe.

- Many with some discretion over their work schedules seem to give greater weight to leisure investments without apology. The concept of a *balance of work and life* now explicitly includes leisure.

  The concept of a *balance of work and life* **now explicitly includes leisure.**

A Review of Continuities and Changes

Continuities in Leisure

- The consistent average 7–8% of household income spent on leisure was consistent until about the year 2000. However, there are three recent changes:

  - The 7% average spending on leisure/recreation narrowly defined gradually rose from 1967 to 2007 to about 11%, suggesting the possibility of a value shift or simply more discretionary income. The percentage spent on government declined from 18 to 13% and food and drink from 17.8 to 10.6%. Therefore some of the change may have been due to decreased costs in other areas (2012).

- However, the recession beginning in 2008 has reduced spending on leisure, especially for those whose employment is uncertain or interrupted.

- Other areas of spending have also increased, especially health care from 8 to 18%. So the competition for budget priority continues.

- One other trend seems to be that there may be increases in leisure spending among the top 10% in income and decreases among the lowest half or so. In summary, overall continuity may have segments of change within the overall percentages.

... primary relationships will remain central to leisure associations and timetables.

• Overall, the core of leisure will still be in accessible activities, especially at home, with outside activities punctuating regular patterns.

• Despite more irregularities in the life course, primary relationships will remain central to leisure associations and timetables.

• Time remains scarce for most adults, but will be more variable.

• The profound changes of the sexual revolution make sexuality and sexual expression recognized as central to leisure meanings and motivations.

• The stylistic elements of play and display are significant themes of most leisure settings.

• Distance costs of away-from-home leisure will continue to increase in congested urban areas.

- Poverty, often intensified by race, produces exclusion from many leisure experiences with alienation evident when the media offer constant images of what the affluent are doing.

- Shopping continues to be a central activity for most across all demographic lines.

- Travel remains important even when styles and costs vary widely.

- Personal leisure investments are an important component of primary relationships for those in committed relationships and those who are not.

- Developmental goals for those raising children are central leisure investments.

- Until the year 2000 every younger cohort has had a higher education level with resulting diversity of leisure experiences and interests.

- The quality of relationships remains central to leisure satisfactions.

- Concerns about the environment may conflict with some recreation uses and developments.

- The trend toward securing blocks of time such as long weekends will continue, especially when the computer offers the possibility of working from almost anywhere.

- The movement toward more independence and self-reliance of women will make their interests and priorities more central to decisions and plans.

Changes in Leisure

- The 50-plus age groups will be recognized as major growing markets for all kinds of goods and services. The "active old" are becoming a primary target market for many leisure businesses.

- Leisure provisions for women will become more diverse and less tied to family.

- The growing "new class" with discretionary income, education, and control over their schedules will attract disproportionate attention from LB developers.

- Off-hour and odd-time leisure will grow with more flexible and irregular work schedules.

- Sunset activities will usually balance new sunrise recreation so that business planners need to be alert to change. For example, the shrinking hunting numbers may be balanced by more backpacking.

- The market sector will come up with more and more leisure implements, programs, toys, and travel offerings, some unrealistic and some on target.

- More adults will be in periods of transition and/or singleness. Diversity in household composition, including sexuality, will be more accepted.

Space scarcities will be more acute ...

- Business offerings will be more central to leisure provisions and will have greater influence on public decisions about land and infrastructure.

- Space scarcities will be more acute, in both public and private environments.

- Home and portable electronics will be more diverse and less costly. Many will fit in well with current lifestyles, but will also attract more expenditures through "planned obsolescence."

- Portability will gain more and more time and attention for communication and entertainment.

- Mass marketing will increase, but leisure diversity will continue and perhaps increase as well.

- Focus on "high-end" clients will saturate many markets, especially as the middle mass commands lower incomes and less purchasing power.

- Reduced public subsidies in areas such as the arts and outdoor resources will open some markets and close others. Reliance on cost recovery by public providers will make business provisions more competitive for some programs and resources.

- Threats to retirement income can reduce both discretionary income and free time for those in traditional retirement periods of life.

- New technologies will impact some activities as fiberglass did to boating and skiing. Not all will be electronic.

- Nonfamily leisure settings and programs will become more common and more central to business marketing.

. . . high-end rentals will flourish.

- Health concerns will be important in leisure choices, especially for those aged 50 and above.

- Travel offerings and packages will become more diverse in response to diverse market segments.

- Many of the more affluent will continue to purchase "big toys" that symbolize their financial status and individualized interests.

- Conversely, some of the affluent will not want to be tied down to particular locales and schedules so that high-end rentals will flourish.

- The skills associated with recreation will become more central to choices and meanings as signs of competence in a world where jobs no longer are signs of ability and even success.

- Employed women will be recognized as a market opportunity equal to men. The bias toward male programs and provisions will largely disappear as a mix of gender-segregated, gender-free, and gender-mixed venues will be sought.

In general, an orientation toward variety and diversity for those with discretionary income will be tempered by the financial limits placed on the majority. Diversity will continue to characterize leisure and provide new business opportunities. A heightened awareness of the importance of leisure to human fulfillment and expression could even change the budget priorities of some individuals and households.

Are the "Small Worlds" Changing?

Yes and no. For the most part, people still live in their immediate environments and with their primary relationships. That means that most leisure is also immediate and with those who are there and convenient. At-home and near-home leisure with household members will continue to dominate time and timetables. Breaking away requires effort and often preplanning.

On the other hand, as repeatedly analyzed, the composition of those small worlds has been changing. Fewer adults and children are in the "traditional" family with two parents and two children. In fact, having children later in life and sending them on their way has reduced the parenting period from 40 years 100 years ago to about 20 IF the family stays intact.

There are two implications for leisure businesses. One is the diversity of primary groups that are the basis of a great deal of leisure. The second is that a very high proportion of adults at any one time are in some period of relationship transition. As discussed, this has implications for marketing and for how a leisure venue is managed and oriented.

Peak Experience, the Real, and the Fake

Of course, any LB has something to sell. However, a central theme of this book is that the "something" isn't really a thing at all. Many business concepts and strategies are focused on what is provided, especially in things that are sold or rented. However, central to the business is the experience. And central to maximizing the experience is what the client is actually doing. Environments are important only as they contribute to the experience. Therefore, it is crucial to know who the clients are, what they hope for, and what they are really doing.

It is possible to argue that the masters of "fakery," the Disney organization, seem to produce a lot of positive experiences where nothing is authentic. One reason probably is that their visitors come expecting the best in fakery and get it. Quality works almost every time. On the other hand, most leisure businesses are designed to attract and keep clients who want to repeat good, and sometimes great, experiences. This means that entertainment is not enough. Leisure clients act and interact in ways that meet their sense of self, expression, ability, and even development. (See Chapters 10 and 11.)

The Question No One Can Answer for You

In the end, all the analysis and possibilities of a leisure business investment and strategy bring the potential entrepreneur back to a more fundamental question that one no one can answer for you.

What Do You Want Your Life to be Like?

If you want security and guarantees, then probably a leisure-based business is not for you. If you want a somewhat open-ended future, involvement with people who are often at their best, the excitement of being able to try out novel possibilities, a sense that what you are doing is uniquely your own, and even the risk of living and working in an open environment, then a LB may what you are seeking. "No one said life would be easy." But the challenge that is met with skill can be central to creating and operating a business as well as to being a satisfied leisure business client. No formulas, but lots of possibilities.

And you will be planning for your own peak experiences as well as for others'.

References

Csikszentmilalyi, M. (1990). *Flow: The Psychology of Optimal Experience.* New York: Harper and Row.

Kelly, J. R. (2012). *Leisure* (4th ed.). Urbana, IL: Sagamore.

Kelly, J. R. (1987). *Peoria Winter: Styles and Resources in Later Life.* Lexington, MA: Lexington Books.

Pine, B. J., & Gilmore, J. H. (1999). *The Experience Economy: Work is Theater, and Every Business a Stage.* Boston, MA: Harvard Business School Press.

Stebbins, R. (1979). *Amateurs: On the Margin Between Work and Leisure.* Beverly Hills, CA: Sage.

About the Author

John R. (Jack) Kelly is Professor Emeritus at the University of Illinois, Urbana-Champaign. He was Professor in Leisure Studies and the Institute for Human Development and Director of the Gerontology and Aging Studies program. His Ph.D. in sociology is from the University of Oregon, and he received masters degrees from Yale, Southern California, and Oregon.

He is author of 11 books including four editions of *Leisure and Recreation Business*, the first text in that field. *Freedom to Be: A New Sociology of Leisure* is a graduate level analysis. He was editor of *Activity and Aging* and coauthor of *Recreation Trends and Markets in the 21st Century* and *21st Century Leisure: Current Issues*. His books have been translated and published in China and Japan. He has authored over 100 research articles, chapters, encyclopedia articles, and technical reports. He has had consulting contracts with American and Japanese corporations including General Motors, Battelle International, and Yamaha as well as the U. S. Forest Service, U.S. Park Service, and State of Illinois.

Among honors he has received are the Roosevelt Research Award, the National Literary Award, and the Distinguished Colleague Award from the National Recreation and Park Association, two research awards from the University of Illinois, and the Nash Scholar prize from the American Association of Leisure and Recreation. He was founding Chair of the Research Commission of World Leisure and has lectured and taught worldwide.